A Psychic in the Heartland

A Psychic in the Heartland

The Extraordinary Experiences
of a Small-Town Doctor

Bettilu Stein Faulkner

Moment Point Press
Portsmouth, New Hampshire

Moment Point Press, Inc.
P.O. Box 4549
Portsmouth, NH 03802-4549
www.momentpoint.com

Cover design by Metaglyph Design and Susan Ray
Typeset in AGaramond
PS

Library of Congress Cataloging-in-Publication Data
Faulkner, Bettilu Stein
A Psychic in the Heartland: the extraordinary
experiences of a small-town doctor / Bettilu Stein Faulkner
p. cm
Includes bibliographical references and index.
ISBN 1-930491-01-8 (pbk. : alk. paper)
1. Hout, Riblet B., 1902–1978.   2. Psychics—Biography.   I. Title.

BF1027.H68 F38 2003
133.8'092—dc21   2002011777

Printed in the United States of America on acid-free paper.

10 9 8 7 6 5 4 3 2

Lovingly dedicated
to the memory of
Riblet B. Hout, D.O.,
and to my three children,
my greatest creative achievements,
Dennis V. Faulkner,
Andrea K. Faulkner, M.D.,
and Cheryl Faulkner Dubois.

How interesting that word death. You on the earth plane shy away from the word, possibly because of misunderstanding. But it is an essential part of life, for change takes place only when one form becomes uninhabitable.

Jules Juret

Contents

Acknowledgments

When I began this project, I worked alone for several years, transcribing over thirty of my uncle Riblet's audiotapes. Around the time I bought my first computer, in 1994, it became apparent that I needed help to complete this book; and the farther I went along, the more help I needed, in a number of ways. I find it difficult, if not impossible, to thank every person who contributed to the creation of this chronicle, but I am particularly indebted to the following people (listed alphabetically). I am most grateful for their support and help in completing this book.

Bruce Bateman, Charles Brennan, Sharon Butler,
Barbara Fuller, John Gialuco, Betsy Hoffman,
Joyce La Judice, Richard Lee, Carole Packer,
Dorothy Parker, Susan Ray, Robert Rippey, Ph.D.,
Millie Schiff, Nancy Painter Scott-Cameron,
Sally Stieber, Lynne Van der Kar, and Hilda Wilkinson

Introduction

A year and a half before his death—or more appropriately, before his *transition*—I visited my uncle Riblet in Florida. As we walked the beach near his home, he told me he would like to pass over. "I could continue my work on that side as well as here," he remarked wistfully. He felt, he said, the presence of his guardian angel, just as he had in his childhood, and he wondered if this was an indication that he was being prepared to leave this plane. "People fear dying because of the unknown," he said. "Many think that when their body has disintegrated, their spirit is dissolved also. If they knew that life continues, as I do, they wouldn't be fearful of taking that step. I look at death as if I were going through a door to a new and wonderful environment, and my belief is that we all have a certain time to leave this world."

Several years later, when asked by an acquaintance why I wanted to write this book, I quoted a few lines contained in a taped letter from my uncle Riblet, one that had never been mailed and had come to me with some of his effects after his death. On the tape, he read to me from his journal an account of one of his out-of-body experiences and said, "That's just one of the experiences that I've had, Betti, which tells me of the continuity of life and the reality of things beyond the physical. If these words will do anyone any good toward easing this passage from death into life—eternal life—feel free to utilize this experience of mine all you care to." It felt to me like a request to tell his story.

And so, this is an account of the life of my late uncle Riblet, a physician, psychic, and healer. Riblet Brisbane Hout (pronounced Howt) was born, raised, and spent most of his life in the conservative Midwest where his psychic abilities were, for practical reasons, known only to a few close friends. Had these talents and activities been generally known in that small town, in the 1920s, in all likelihood he would have been ostracized and unable to practice his profession.

Uncle Rib was tall, handsome, and charming. As a child, I adored him. He was my hero, and somewhat of a father figure. During his frequent visits to my parents' home, my three siblings and I delighted in Uncle Rib's undivided attention. Living as we were in the gray Depression era, whenever his Model A pulled into view, there was always great excitement—his visits brought a ray of sunshine to our lives. Whether the occasion was a picnic on a summer's day or a holiday get-together, Rib's natural buoyancy and enthusiasm permeated our entire family. When I went off to nursing school, it was Rib who drove me to the city, and who treated me to dinner in a fine restaurant whenever he visited.

A man of modest, Midwestern tastes and unfailing good humor, Uncle Rib taught me the advantage of an optimistic outlook and the blessings of simple pleasures. One anecdote he liked to tell reveals his spirited nature and good heart. "One time I had a female patient who needed a series of treatments," he told us. "I knew the minute I touched her that she'd never pay me, but I thought, 'Well, I can treat her anyway.' I also knew she *could* pay because I was aware she had insurance. So I treated her a number of times and she got back to normal living. Then she came in one day and said, 'You know, Dr. Hout, I don't intend to pay you for the treatments. I have insurance and I got the money from the insurance company, but I just used it to buy a new washing machine!'"

"And I knew long before she told me," he laughed. "Wasn't that funny? At least she was honest enough to come in and tell me she bought the washing machine."

As I grew up, I realized Rib, like all humans, had his faults—he was somewhat self-centered and liked to be in control of things—but my admiration for him never flagged, even though I lived hundreds of miles away and visits became rare. In a letter to my mother sent the day after his death, I wrote, "His many visits and his interest in us kids provided an enrichment that is, without a doubt, impossible to appreciate."

In 1977, a year before he passed over, I took a course called "Dreams and Altered States of Consciousness" for which I wrote a comprehensive term paper on out-of-body experiences. Uncle Rib, realizing my interest in such topics, sent me his journal. And with that, I learned for the first time of the happenings of his extraordinary life.

Although he experienced metaphysical events from his earliest childhood, his amazing out-of-body experiences occurred with the guidance of his spirit guide, George Felbers. While in his early thirties, Rib first met George in an unusual psychic episode that borders on the whimsical (and is detailed in chapter 2). Hoping—and perhaps intuitively realizing—that he would have out-of-body experiences, Rib purchased a small, red, hard-backed journal and faithfully wrote down what had transpired immediately after the close of each encounter. He had an artistic bent, and his observations were written in a slightly florid style, typical of his time. As a result, the careful descriptions of the things he experienced and saw allows the reader to vividly picture what it's like on that other side.

Having planned ahead of time the destinations for these out-of-body trips, George, Rib's spirit guide and mentor, accompanied his pupil to wondrous places and mystical planes. Not only did Rib visit his beloved mother and other relatives who had died, but also former patients, old friends, and spirit teachers. Indeed, the incredible spirit conferences he observed revealed not only the ways in which we who inhabit the earth plane are the beneficiaries of such meetings, but also that we do indeed have a connection with that other side—if we but recognize it.

In addition to the treasured journal, Rib left behind many audiotapes of his thoughts and also interviews with some of his patients, friends, and his sister, Helen—my mother, and his only sibling. He also left behind psychic photographs—photographs in which spirit entities appear— with explanations of the circumstances under which they were made. He left a number of clippings from spiritualist newspapers, some of which reported his arrival at spiritual communities in New York, southern Indiana, and Florida. His mission at these assemblies was, in the main, to share what he had learned from George and from his own out-of-body experiences. He lectured, taught classes, took part in séances, and socialized, all in addition to treating his regular patients.

Rib's psychic talent extended to his work as a physician and resulted in numerous healings, as described by patients, friends, relatives, and the doctor himself. And these healing talents were also discussed, at various times, by George. Perhaps the most important items left by Riblet, in fact, were the audiotaped messages from George. Rib accomplished these recordings by first setting up the tape recorder, and then, by means of self hypnosis, going into a trance and allowing his spirit guide to speak through him. George explained fascinating spiritual truths—what we experience at the moment of death, life and work on the other side, and the nature of his and Riblet's work in previous incarnations. George also discussed fate, free will, destiny, and God.

As my uncle's closest relative, my mother inherited all of her brother's personal effects after his passing. Knowing of my interest in these matters, she turned over to me all of Rib's tapes, clippings, letters, and other materials. While writing a book was not on my mind at that time, eventually I felt compelled to do so. As might be imagined, the task of compiling, transcribing, and organizing all of these materials took many years. Nevertheless, I was determined to see it through. I've always felt strongly about making this material available to anyone and everyone who is interested. Perhaps this book is simply an extension of my uncle's work in another era.

In talking to Rib's friends, relatives, acquaintances, and patients, it was obvious that throughout his life, this gentle man made a great deal of difference in the lives of the many people he touched. His healings, his compassionate counseling, physically and spiritually, made a positive difference in the lives of those to whom he gave guidance. And his knowledge of life after death certainly influenced our family. At the time of my youngest brother Dick's death, in his forties, for example, his pastor and the funeral director let it be known that Dick's planning and courage in facing his passing was like no other they had seen.[1] In fact, none of Rib's nieces or nephews, including myself, ever feared death.

The riddle of what happens to the human spirit after we die has, by turns, frightened, intrigued, and mystified mankind. While my fervent wish is to help people overcome their fear of death, it is also my hope that the revelations contained in this book will grant the reader a deeper understanding of the soul's progression and invincibility. Those who are open to such ideas may well find some inspiration relating to the eternal question, "What is life all about?"

I am happy to share Rib's story—and for the most part, I have tried to let Riblet and George tell their own story. No matter how many times I've read of my uncle's psychic adventures, I never fail to get as excited as I did upon the first reading. I hope my readers feel the same way.

chapter 1

THE BOY
WHO WAS DIFFERENT

On the last day of September, 1902, in the small farming community of Middlebury, Indiana, Cora Riblet Hout gave birth to her second child. Christened Riblet Brisbane, this boisterous infant was cause for great joy in the Hout household. Already the parents of a five-year-old daughter, Cora and her husband, Solomon, had long yearned for another child—preferably a boy. Had they known they were welcoming a psychic medium into their midst, they may well have greeted their newborn son with apprehension.

As it was, surrounded by Amish farms and within hiking distance of the Elkhart River and Michigan border, Riblet spent an idyllic childhood in a village in northern Indiana, playing in the village square across the street from the home where he was born. Self-sufficient Hoosiers, born of pioneer stock, Sol and Cora were politically conservative, God-fearing English-Lutherans, the embodiment of turn-of-the-century, Midwestern ideals. Séances, spirit materializations, and out-of-body experiences were as alien to the Houts' Christian tenets as Hinduism would have been. Belief in the supernatural was deemed an aberrant psychological affliction, and anyone holding such beliefs was considered "different." As one Middlebury native describes it, "Folks who practiced mysticism kept their beliefs to themselves or risked being ostracized—maybe even sent to an asylum." So, early on, Rib, a naturally gregarious, outspoken youngster, strove to keep his peace.

"I saw strange beings on a regular basis as a child," he recounted. "They appeared in many forms—fairies, elves, angels, gnomes, sylphs, and salamanders. Finding that the little people mostly liked to be around growing things, I often climbed my favorite tree and played with them. My psychic force must have attracted these playful spirits to me—afforded them energy, perhaps. It was clear from their antics that these phantoms reveled in the fact that I could see them."[1]

Afraid of what mischief the spirits might unleash in the dark of night, Rib pleaded, "Mama, tuck in the bedclothes and leave the lamp lit." When Cora questioned why this bedtime ritual was necessary, five-year-old Rib explained, "The little people might climb up and get me while I sleep."

Assuming, perhaps, that Rib was just experiencing normal childhood "boogeyman" fears, Cora didn't argue her small son's logic or even inquire as to who these "little people" might be. Years later, Rib was unable to recall whether or not he openly discussed the antics of the little people with his family. He did remember, however, that as a five-year-old he informed a neighbor of what he saw and was scolded for his tale of "seeing a goblin."

Another neighbor recalled Riblet as an ordinary little boy growing up in the early 1900s. In a charming letter sent to my mother in 1964, the neighbor whose family, including their daughter Mabel, had been close friends with the Houts, wrote:

> You folks were our best neighbors. I have a picture of Mabel and Riblet going to Sunday School. Riblet had a white suit on trimmed in blue. Mabel had a white dress on trimmed in blue. They were holding hands. I don't think they were over five or six years old. Your mother and I had go-carts for them. One Sunday we went to the cemetery for Memorial Day. While we were [there] it started to rain. So we went back to the church. Your mother and I had to sit in the aisle and hold the children. When we got home your mother came over and said, 'What do you think I did?' She said she took Riblet [into church] without any pants! She had hung them on the oven door and forgot to put them on!

But although he shared typical childhood experiences with his little friends, Rib was learning that he wasn't quite the same as they. Being different isn't easy for any child, and Rib was no exception. He was, by all accounts, an outgoing child, but whose principal mainstay was Cora. Whether or not she approved, or even shared her son's psychic precociousness, is a matter of conjecture. It is known, however, that she seemed more tolerant of psychic phenomena than most people of her day and did little to dissuade her son's budding interest in it. Indeed, it was Cora who reported her own supernatural experience to Rib when he was older.

"Mother enjoyed weaving fabrics of her own design," Rib recounted years later. "An artistic and intuitive person, she'd take a lantern out to the barn at night, to work over a large loom. She'd hang the flickering kerosene lamp on a hook overhead and, with no evidence of a breeze or disturbance in the barn, the heavy lantern would sway gently, back and forth, the entire time she worked. When she told me about the lantern's movement, it was clear that she considered it something out of the ordinary."

Rib also explained that his mother accepted New Thought, a mental healing movement whose philosophy includes the idea that man is a manifestation of God, and therefore possesses the power to create and heal with the mind.[2] Cora also regularly read *Nautilus* magazine,[3] whose religious articles clearly did not correspond with any established religion. *Nautilus*, which ceased publication in 1953, was edited by Elizabeth Towne, a prolific New Thought writer, and included articles on science, psychology, telepathy, auras, clairvoyance and natural healing, among other topics. The fact that Cora subscribed to this magazine may provide a clue to her interest in mysticism.

Sol, on the other hand, tolerated none of what he termed, "Rib's shenanigans." "Because of the psychic energy that I had no control of," Rib explained, "I got in trouble more with my father, who was always threatening me. My worst fear as a child was my dad coming after me. All of a sudden, I would see flashes of color around myself, feel something like a vortex whirling me into nothingness. It was very intense and most unpleasant. Those episodes were the unhappiest times of my childhood, but fortunately, as I grew older, they disappeared."

"My father was a fair, but stern man," Rib allowed. Sol was a lean-muscled, no-nonsense taskmaster, a telephone-company employee who worked from dawn till dusk selling telephone service and installing phones to new subscribers across the Indiana countryside. Later, he moved his family from Middlebury to the nearby town of Goshen, where he bought and operated a grocery store.

"When I was in my teens, " Rib said, "poltergeist activity was a real problem. Not understanding it, I didn't have very good control of the pent-up psychic energy; and Dad often accused me of being deliberately disobedient, when I hadn't been. I remember he once asked me to pump a pail of water which then tipped over on him without my touching it. He was enraged, yelling, 'You're going to take my foot'— a vernacular expression he used when he was angry—and started toward me. Of course I got punished. I remember another time I was at the top of the basement stairs, and he was at the bottom. Suddenly a small board that was standing on the top step, leaning against the wall, went hurtling downstairs of its own accord. I hadn't touched it! But of course Dad thought I was responsible."

A habitual sleepwalker in his teens, Rib sometimes roamed the house at night. Accustomed to encountering spirits in the corridors, his typical reaction was nonchalance, but one incident in particular disturbed him. Waking thirsty late one night, Rib wandered downstairs to the kitchen for a drink. Standing at the sink, he tried to draw water from the well and was startled to see his hand go right through the pump handle. Pondering the episode later, he realized he had been out of his body. "I was astral projecting, trying to get a drink of water, and I couldn't because I'd left my body upstairs!"

Another time, Rib nearly collided with an apparition. "This gave me pause. Usually the spirits were misty in appearance, but this one looked mortal. It didn't dawn on me until much later that, when I was in my astral body, the spirits looked solid, but when I was in my physical body, the spirits were semitransparent."

A popular youth who amused his chums with poetry readings, impromptu plays, and magic shows, Rib gained a reputation for being the class clown.

"As a kid," he admitted, "I was a blatant showoff and did a lot of dramatic, hocus-pocus stuff, but it was all in fun. I was performing sleight of hand one afternoon, with my sister and some neighbor kids for my audience. The nearby French doors leading to the empty parlor were closed, but

14

there was a rug under the doors that was partly in the room where we were. I was standing on it but when I stepped off the small carpet, before I could say abracadabra, the rug flew under the door, clear into the next room. All us kids tore out of the house screaming. I didn't try any more magic tricks for a long time."

Despite his sleepwalking and strange sightings, Rib succeeded in school. "Teachers seemed to understand me somehow; they were kind. I don't give myself credit for super intelligence, but in grammar school and throughout high school, I got As and Bs without really trying. Lessons came easy because, in examinations, I would write answers to questions I didn't know. I guess someone up there was helping me."

Conscious of his guardian angel since childhood, Rib said, "I couldn't see his face, just the outline of his body. He never spoke a word and, to this day, I have no idea who he might have been, except that I knew he was my protector, my buffer. He had a regalness about him and always stood at my right side, but behind me. I accepted him as casually as I accept you—as casually as any trusting child. He was with me all through high school and when I no longer detected his presence, I realized I had taken his devotion for granted."

Much later, Rib came to rely on his spirit guides in much the same way he had his guardian angel, but, he said, "I never had any doubt that this, my first protector, was special—different from all those that followed."

In addition to the gradual departure of his guardian angel, two events occurred in Rib's senior year that would determine the direction of his life.

Able to discern auras surrounding the ill and infirm, Rib felt a keen empathy for the sick and suffering. When his grandmother Riblet became seriously ill, his only consolation was the fact that her aura did not indicate death. "Her colors weren't muddy," he explained, "they were bright."

Worried nonetheless, the family called in a respected female osteopath. Gradually, the grandmother's condition improved and Sol and Cora, impressed with the doctor's diagnostic skills and her powers of healing, voiced their gratitude. When the doctor commented that Rib had all the necessary requisites to become a physician himself, the family discussed the possibility. Cora and Sol had fancied the ministry for their son, but they were soon swayed by Rib's enthusiasm for a medical career. And so, with his parents' consent, Rib applied to the American School of Osteopathy in Kirksville, Missouri.[4]

It's important here to understand the difference between a traditional American medical practice and osteopathy. Developed in the late nineteenth century, osteopathic medicine is a unique form of American medical care that focuses on the unity of all body parts and recognizes the body's ability to heal itself. Osteopathy also stresses preventive medicine, eating properly, and keeping fit. In effect, osteopathy is responsible for the modern-day concept we call wellness.

An osteopath, in practice, evaluates patients' personal health risks and then acts as a teacher to help them take more responsibility for their own well-being by changing unhealthy patterns. In other words, osteopaths practice a "whole person" approach to medicine rather than treating specific symptoms or illnesses only. And incorporated into the osteopath's practice is the osteopathic manipulative treatment—known by patients as, simply, a "treatment"—in which physicians use their hands to diagnose injury and illness and to encourage the body's natural tendency toward good health.[5]

It is not surprising, then, given Riblet's psychic experiences, in his youth and throughout his life, that he would have been drawn to osteopathy. In fact, as we shall learn, it is precisely Riblet's psychic abilities and his ability to heal by touch, that allowed him to bring such profound relief to his patients.

In the same year that Riblet applied to medical school, he discovered, on a routine visit to the library, a very special book. There, on a dusty shelf, he came across a dog-eared volume by Sir Arthur Conan Doyle entitled, *Wanderings of a Spiritualist*.[6] Rib enthusiastically read accounts of ordinary people experiencing supernatural visitations and occurrences similar to his own.

"I'm not the only one," he excitedly told his best friend, Charles Brennan. "There are other people who see what I see." Charles, a chum Riblet met when they both took part in little theater productions, was a methodical, prudent person. Although not as outgoing as Riblet, he was a loyal and supportive friend. In fact, it seemed meant to be that Charles would be the one who would help Rib understand his mystical experiences. It so happened that in Charles's home was an entire collection of books on psychic phenomena—and Charles kindly asked his parents' permission for Rib to borrow them. The collection was actually a small library that belonged to a group of his father's friends.

As it turned out, Charles, who'd never so much as hinted that his father was a devotee of spiritualism, regularly attended séances, meetings where people attempted to receive messages from the spirit world. Rib was ecstatic when he was invited to join the group in a session with a medium who specialized in materialization—that is the ability to produce a spirit in a form visible to the human eye. As he recalled it, "I remember the séance took place in semidarkness in the medium's home. She sat behind a curtain, which opened and closed, according to the whims of the spirits, who appeared one after another." Rib saw them all, but recognized none until, standing before him, was the image of his loving grandfather, John P. K. Riblet, who had died five years earlier.

"Everyone in the room saw Grandpa," Rib recalled, "but no one reacted like I did. It frightened the life out of me! He stepped toward me and tried to touch me. Terrified, I backed up—too frightened to speak. His long white beard and facial features were just as I'd remembered him. There was no doubt in my mind who this was." Despite this apprehensive reunion, Rib was overjoyed that the medium had contacted his beloved grandfather. And with this experience, the terrible loneliness and fear of ridicule with which he had suffered in silence for so long subsided somewhat. He had compatriots—fellow pilgrims voyaging into unorthodox realms. He saw mysticism as a gift to be explored and celebrated. Poring over textbooks, periodicals, and literature, Rib pledged to dedicate his life to studying this thing called spiritualism.

chapter 2

EARLY MESSAGES
FROM BEYOND

After high school graduation, Rib took a year's hiatus and worked alongside Sol and Cora in the grocery store, saving every dollar he earned. In the autumn of 1921, waving goodbye to family, friends, and his high school sweetheart, he set out for the long journey to Missouri and medical school. As the train pulled away from the depot, he knew he was heading too far from home to return for weekend visits, but he arrived in Kirksville determined to apply himself to the studies needed for entrance into the healing profession. While he wasn't active in the school's extracurricular programs, he learned, through some women students from a nearby teachers' college, about a little theater group and was invited to participate. He was pleased to find he enjoyed the stage.

During his college years, Riblet also met, through correspondence only, the sister of a classmate, and fell in love. Although he longed to meet her in person, this was not to be. The young woman suddenly fell ill and died shortly after an operation. Because he felt that she was the only girl for him, this was a devastating blow to the young student. But while he grieved, he kept up his work, realizing the need to remain true to his goal. The seasons and semesters flew by, and, in June of 1925, Riblet was graduated from medical school, being awarded the degree, Doctor of Osteopathy. Shortly afterward, he took and passed the state medical boards, and was granted a license to practice.

Diploma in hand, he returned to Goshen and was greeted at the station by his parents, my mother, my sister, and me. The house, his mother's large flower garden, and even Main Street, looked the same, yet so much in Riblet's young life had changed. His best friend, Charles, had accepted a job in Chicago, his high school sweetheart was now married, and Sol and Cora had sold the grocery store.

Shaking off the unexplained loneliness that haunted him since childhood, Rib purchased a few essential pieces of medical equipment and sent out announcements that he was starting a practice. "My equipment and shingle very nearly got cloaked in cobwebs," Rib laughed. "It seemed the townsfolk balked at consulting a twenty-three-year-old doctor for their medical problems. If I had been renting an office, I would have had to give up sooner."

Before long, he repacked his bags, and with medical equipment in tow, headed for Illinois. "My friend, Charles," he explained, "had a good paying job with a utility company in the suburbs of Chicago and he invited me to join him there. I set up a small practice, placing ads in all the newspapers. The problem was, patients would take one look at my youthful face and ask, 'Where's the doctor?' It infuriated me.

"What little money we earned between us saw us through the winter, but in the spring, the power plant laid Charles off. My patient fees weren't enough to carry us both, so we headed back home to Indiana." So just six months after Rib left Goshen, he returned, again setting up an office in his parents's home. He had always been more in touch with his mother than with his father. Now, with his office in the home, mother and son had ample opportunity to converse and share ideas. Cora was proud of her only son's progress in his chosen field, and they became even closer. But, just when all seemed right with Rib's world, it fell apart.

One cold winter day in 1927, just shortly after Riblet had brought her to visit my mother and the rest of my family, Cora contracted quinsy, a severe tonsil infection. Since this was more than two decades before the discovery of penicillin or other antibiotics, Rib stayed at his mother's bedside, using every bit of knowledge and skill he could muster. He administered the best medications of the day and gave her osteopathic treatments. He called on colleagues and brought in a specialist. But it was all for naught. The deadly infection raged and spread, resulting in spinal meningitis. Two weeks after she first became ill, Rib's cherished mother, only fifty-five years old, died and was laid to rest in the family plot. Despite his mother's assurance that they would meet again in the afterlife, Rib was inconsolable.

He had been grappling within himself about life. Putting his thoughts on paper, he wrote, "I longed to link up my native intelligence with a substantial outlook on life that really could satisfy me deep within. I wanted so much to believe and understand and know. I now wanted to know what had become of my precious mother, and whether she was still alive—was she happy? If she really continued to live, what was she doing and experiencing? Did she miss me as much as I missed her?" The answers to these questions came in an unexpected but profound way a few months later.

Distraught by grief, Rib sought solace by turning to the psychic material he had read over the years, and to his friend Charles. Death, they reminded him, was not the end, but merely a bridge to another life filled with love, learning, and wonderful experiences. But how could he find the way to cross over that bridge? Relying on the determination, stamina, and perseverance that Cora herself had instilled in him, Rib immersed himself in the study of psychic phenomena and meditation. He also practiced the art of automatic writing, a process that involves letting the mind be passive while the hand, lightly holding a pen or pencil, receives and writes down messages from the spirit world. Within a few short months of practice, he received his first message. It was from Cora, his devoted mother:

My Son,
I am so very happy to be able to write to you. I want to tell you what a happy home I have here sur-

24

rounded by loved ones and kept busy with loving duties. My home is a white marble and alabaster mansion. At least you would call it that. The carvings are most magnificent on the doorways and on the walls. I do my own decorating with beautiful things that I design myself. I do this, for I often entertain children and others. We never need to rest over here but I have a resting room reserved for those who wish it—strangers from your plane are sometimes brought here as I help them get accustomed to the location.

I am here with Grandpa, Ella, Ida [Cora's sisters], and Mother, and I am often in your presence when you do not know it. I was there in the room with you and Dad and Helen many times before they laid my body away and I was so very sorry for your grief.

I am entirely happy. This place where I am is too beautiful to describe and all is filled with love. The very air we breathe is love and the nearer perfect we become in our love, the nearer we come to perfection. My boy, you cannot comprehend God's love and magnitude. Even we who are here can only sense faintly His greatness.

You were right when you said the churches didn't have true religion and you were right when you said God gave us our brains to reason things out. But you were wrong when you said that we didn't have divine help, for I now know that God's influence, through His angels, comes to you daily, hourly, constantly. Lately, you are beginning to learn that fact to your own satisfaction, aren't you?

We who love you are helping you and we will help you many times more. However, I won't teach you. Your guides can do that better than I. I can only tell you that I am still gloriously alive and so happy and full of joy.

My son, I had to "die" to learn the lessons that God, through His love, wanted me to learn. If you can learn them early in life, it will help you so much more. When I was called home, I was met at the door of my new dwelling by Ella and Pa and they taught me to be active and busy over here.

I was impressed by the beautiful light that you carry around with you, and I was told it is the light of spiritual understanding that will soon envelop you. You are to be given more instructions by the higher teachers and that is the occasion of my joy today. This is my first opportunity to control your hand to write, and I love to do it. It gives me such a sense of material nearness to you. But I am tiring you and I don't want to do that.

Your wonderful guide is helping me get this long letter through to you. I will write again soon. See, I am getting stronger all the time.

All my love to you, my son.

Mother

The following year, Rib, in talking to a friend about his mother and her contact with him since her passing, explained, "My mother has written me several letters, with automatic writing, telling about her reaction to her death. It was so different from what I thought it was. I was with her when she died, but at that time I didn't see any psychic activity. I was too emotionally involved, of course."

Shortly after Rib received his mother's message, George, the discarnate being who would eventually lead Rib to strange new worlds and countless self-discoveries, appeared suddenly and without warning. Where? On the stage, of course.

"I was in my twenties," Rib recalled, "and being fond of classical music, I attended a concert. Engrossed in the melody, I caught a dazzle—a flash of light out of the corner of my eye. Looking around, I noticed a young man with a mop of reddish hair playing a violin near the wings. Drawing his bow over the strings, he stood cross-legged. It was kind of a crazy stance and it occurred to me, 'this must be a spirit,' although he looked solid enough. When the violinist saw he had my attention, he smiled, playing louder and faster. I left the theater questioning my own sanity. A few days later I attended a séance, and the first voice that came through said, 'Well, you saw me with my violin, didn't you?' He introduced himself, saying, 'My name is George Felbers, and we're going to work together.' "

Within a week of their first meeting, Rib received a letter, via automatic writing, from this strange and splendid man who referred to himself as Rib's "spirit guide."

My Dear Buddy,

I have been with you for about two years now and I am very much interested in you and all your activities. Please understand that what I tell you is merely an introductory sketch to serve as background for the work that will follow.

First, I want you to know that I am a natural being, and I have my duties to perform even as you have. You are interested in a religious motive dealing with practical transcendent ideas. Not only am I also interested in those things, I am experiencing them; and I find myself placed in the plane toward which you are seeking.

It is all very logical, isn't it? Several of us are here at one end of the inter-plane telephone wire and you are at the other. When proper connections are made by our two central offices, I speak very naturally to you; and you, with some misgivings, voice back mentally to me. If I am able to prove to you my actual objective reality and you tune in with vigor and desire, it makes the connection that much better.

In short, I am ready to begin work with you and I am appreciative that you have made conditions easier for us to voice to you. You have it within your power to cut the connection or relay a busy signal so, for those standing near me now, I want to voice my thanks for your cooperation.

I want to stress the naturalness of it all over here. Our bodies are attuned to our vibratory environment even as your body is attuned to physical matter. We live in accordance with the law of harmony and we utilize certain senses to orient ourselves, even as you do. We live, we are natural, even to the point of forgetting occasionally, that we have lived anywhere but here.

We are also variously active. We do not wander aimlessly among the flowers, chasing butterflies, for we have work to do. We choose the things we want to do and, as a result, we are happy in our work.

Since I have always loved music, I have followed through with that and, as I also see a need for pioneering methods of communication, I apply myself to getting the truth across. We are alive after death, we go on, doing the things we want to do and should do.

You and I will be working in partnership, each with our separate work and environment. We are each in a certain portion of God's great universe, each for a particular purpose. That is, of course, that we may learn certain things. For only by learning may we progress. And only by progression may we come nearer to perfection.

I know for a fact, there are highly evolved souls who are much nearer the point of perfection than I. I long with a real soul longing to master the truths that are around and about me. I want to carry with me the glory that I have seen reflected in the faces of saints that I have imperfectly seen through my imperfect vision. There is so much for us all to learn how to live fuller, more perfect lives and I wonder that more folks don't realize this fact.

But, of course, each one must find out these things for himself. It isn't that I can tell you all about this life toward which you are heading and can prepare you, but it is that you must experience for yourself and learn your lessons your own way. Only then will you become a part of your own soul.

I work here with a research group interested in exploring certain truths that we feel are pertinent. One member of my group is called Bill, and it was through his efforts that I met your mentor. Since I have been permitted to work with you, I am indeed optimistic and see much promise for the future.

I believe we should stop now, but I will follow this effort with more work of a similar nature, if you so desire. I'm sure the scientific aspects of our group's plans will be of interest to you. Also, I want you to meet the members of our group.

I bid you adieu,

George

Reading and rereading this letter gave Rib cause for deep concern. What if these words were merely figments of his own imagination or subconscious mind? Could he believe that a disembodied entity was busy making plans for them to work together? Was it possible that the so-called dead were actually leading lives not so different from his own in another dimension? Was this communication the answer to his own soul's abiding loneliness and longing?

If he embraced and openly espoused such an unconventional philosophy, how would it impact his lifestyle, his profession? Wasn't the scientific mind and training of a physician in direct conflict with tenets of spiritualism? Remembering the ridicule he'd endured when telling a neighbor of his childhood visits with elves and fairies, Rib felt his feet go cold. It was one thing to attend séances in darkened rooms out of the public eye and quite another to openly adopt the practice of mysticism. Religious persecution and prejudice were alive and well in the heartland of the 1930s.

"What to do, what to do?" The question tormented him day and night.

"Wait for a sign. Wait and see what happens next," were the words that popped into his head again and again.

chapter 3

A Picture of Life
on the Other Side

Rib didn't have long to wait for a sign. Poring over books written by authors who had themselves experienced astral projections—or as they are also known, out-of-body experiences—he read about the methods of going out-of-body, actually taking the time to meditate about this and practice the technique. Falling into a light trance one evening, he felt a strange sensation and, upon opening his eyes, found himself at the ceiling, looking down at the furniture and objects in the room: the easy chair with his sleeping body, the bed, the desk piled with books, and his box of pencils. One thing particularly caught his eye: the little red hard-backed book—with empty pages—that he had purchased for recording his hoped for out-of-body experiences.

A few days later, while meditating about his friends and family who had died, Rib was filled with wistful emotion. He asked the guides to show him the way to break through to the other side. Instantly, George appeared.

"He asked whether or not I would follow where he led me," Rib explained, "and, of course, I said, 'Yes.'"

The Concentration Room Experience

Place: Alone in my room. Time: 2:45 P.M. to 3:15 P.M. George comes and aids me to leave my body. I am conscious of the separation of two parts; we pass through doors into the spirit plane from the material plane. The doors

Riblet's sketch of the doors

are solid, and I can feel waves of material substance between us and the physical body.

We enter the concentration room, where are Mother, aunts Ada, Ida, and Ella, and Grandfather Riblet.[1] The room is round with a domed ceiling. The room is softly lighted, indirectly. Tables, davenports, and rugs furnish the room. In the center is a table on which is a crystal-clear ball of light. All are centering their attention on it. This changes color slowly. First it is white, then soft yellow, rose, then violet. I stand in the room but am invisible until the light turns to violet. Then George and I both are seen [by the others in the room]. This causes great pull on my spirit, back to the physical. I withstand it and then we converse.

Then the teacher of the group appears. I see her as the Madonna of the Lily. She is dressed in white and gold with a round headdress. She has a white halo with a gold band. She speaks and welcomes me and tells of the work I am to do. As she fades away from view, Cyrius [a teacher][2] fades in, wearing purple. He speaks.

Then I feel the pull to my body become stronger, and I was forced back to the doors with George. I gain more strength, and we return. I learn more about the group and their plans and life and work, and then return to the body.

I awake in the body, with George standing by my side.

Rib was filled with emotion as he contemplated his experience. While he had read about leaving one's body, he had never imagined in his wildest dreams that he would be able to see such beauty or feel such peace. The ease with which he'd been able to shed his physical body to visit these loving beings on another plane convinced him that man's eternal quest for God was not rooted in archaic lore, but rather in universal reality. It struck Rib that spiritual enlightenment is the soul's birthright.

Later, as he matured spiritually, he was helped more than he realized—now able to recognize George's presence from time to time. While shopping for phonograph records one day, he noticed a good quality tape recorder and decided to purchase it, thinking it would be a kind of toy. In a subsequent message, George told Riblet that it was he who had impressed Rib to buy the tape machine. Spending an evening with some close friends the following weekend, it was suggested that Riblet might go into trance using the recorder in the event any of his spirit friends wished to speak to the group. The small audience wasn't disappointed; George spoke and gave specific instructions to Riblet, reminding him of their plan to work together. Finding a quiet time, Riblet was to set up the recorder at his bedside, lie on his bed with the microphone at hand, and go into trance so that George could speak through him, sending him messages that could be preserved.

Rib was excited at this prospect, wondering what his guide would have to say. Wasting no time, that very night he plugged the microphone into the recorder and lay down on his bed with great anticipation. After a few introductory words, he easily fell into trance by using a deep-breathing technique. And true to his word, George spoke through Rib, describing his life on the other side.

George's World

RIBLET: The time is 11:15 P.M. I'm in bed relaxing, with the microphone in my hand, and feeling the presence of George and the nearness of him. I'm being impressed with the thought that he would like to speak about life in his world, the spirit world, the plane of life which is close enough to come into contact with the physical plane whenever he wishes, but far enough away to enhance his spiritual value.

GEORGE: Dear Riblet, I do come to you with the purpose of attempting to tell you something of my life over here where I am, in the spirit world. You realize that I am a being apart from you, living a life that is wholly unfamiliar to you, but one which can give you great joy and happiness to contact. My world is real, Riblet, just as real as is your world. To you, stone is a very solid substance. A stone or a tree and my general environment is as solid and real to me as is yours to you, the difference being that the environment in which I find myself is amenable to manipulation. It is reactive to the power of thought, subtle in ways you cannot comprehend. I live almost in the immediate now, and I can change my environment at almost an instant's notice. My world is composed more nearly of molecules of light, which are transmitted and made into forms through the power of thought.

Where you live, the law of cause and effect reigns in a matter of timing. You are surrounded by a series of vibrations of low intensity and slow reaction, so that you may reap the harvest of experience and understanding. If you can accept this as being so, you can understand how the physical plane of life manifests itself, according to the law of cause and effect. The cause is thrown out into the ether, usually as a thought wave. It becomes dynamic in the universal ether, according to the atomic usage, and it radiates or vibrates, or scintillates in such a manner as to attract to itself the things which are harmonious to it, and put away from it the inimical or unfriendly things which are of the opposite order.

We know that your plane of life reacts in substance which is slow of reaction. That is as it should be, for there is where you experience; there is where you grow with spirit consciousness;

there is where you struggle and learn, weep and try again, and gradually adjust yourself to the existing conditions. That is needed for the power of Spirit to become dominant within your lifetime on the earth plane. Over here, those things are needless.

I remember when I first came over here, two particular things brought me into a consciousness of surprise and almost shock. First was the luminosity of the world I had entered. I had never seen anything like it. A tree would bear a light within itself, if you can comprehend the words as I mean them to be. A tree would glow and I seemed to know it was a glow of spiritual power, of divine energy, of universal force.

Where I am, a tree scintillates light. It gives a feeling of stability in its thrust of spiritual energy as seen by light. I didn't know what to make of the luminosity of various objects as I saw them, immediately after I came over here. I didn't realize at that particular time that I had died, and was living in a different plane of life than I'd ever lived in before.

I would have you know that we are alive and active and interested in what goes forth from our united world, same as are you. I would like to have you comprehend the construction of the bridge of light between the worlds and have you know and realize the reality of the two worlds, of the double thread of which you are reading, and of the reality of the invisible, as the power of your life.

I think myself to where I wish to be. I think myself into an environment that is harmonious to me. When I wish to will myself into the silence or the golden light or the true power of

Spirit, I have but to become quiet, turning my thoughts inward, and transport myself and my thinking to the world where I wish to be.

We have fewer hindrances along the way. We are inspired by more nearly perfect spiritual attunement with life than are you. We have fewer difficulties, we have fewer intrusions of matter, and more spiritual dominance of power regarding mental reaction and spiritual enlightenment.

Anyway, I will try to explain to you something of the world in which I live and the way I live it. The plane of life on which I live is what we choose to call the Summerland. That is to say, I am living in a plane of life where light is a dominant factor of my existence. Light infiltrates and infuses every living thing within our realm of being.

The Summerland is a great realm of life which is like the physical plane in natural beauty. I am living in a vast valley surrounded by beautiful, magnificent mountains. And I can look out to see lakes, beautiful forests, and magnificent flowers everywhere. For my abode, I have chosen a type of dwelling that you might call a Swiss Chalet, a two-story structure. My home is arranged for rest, for recreation, and for joy of meditation. I am living in a manner similar to that in which you live except that there is a quality of refinement and finesse about my realm that you would notice. The room in which I spend much of my time, and where I greet my friends, is arranged like a living room, perhaps. It is filled with furnishings of softness and beauty of line and color, and since I'm working on the purple ray,[3] which is like the teacher that we are accustomed to, I have chosen colors harmonious with purple and gold. Each thing is infused with its own interior luminosity, but it isn't like a light which shines from one of your lamps. External light, such as the sun or electric lights, is not needed here.

Then there is my meditation room where I may go for quiet, peace, prayer, greater understanding, and more uplift. There is the room of repose where I may quiet myself in thought, and breathe into my being some of God's great energy. I can partake of this through thought, through food if necessary, and through repose of sleep or quiet time. These things are essential to us even as they are to you. We accept them in perhaps a more refined manner, but in a way which would be responsive to your understanding if you were over here living with me now.

In saying these things to you, I am attempting to adapt my plane of life into an understanding that you can accept through words of your phrasing and through your mind, Riblet. It is sometimes difficult for me to express myself clearly and correctly because there may be no exact duplication of phrases. I do want you to know that I, as a living being, have my needs for a harmonious environment even as do you. My world is a real world, however, just as real to me as your world is to you though you don't comprehend that.

I can reach out my hand and feel substance just as you can feel the table beside you or the davenport upon which you sometimes sit to meditate. I can reach out and pull to me objects that are real and solid, just as objects are real and solid to you on the physical plane. But apart from that, through the manipulation of thought force, through the power of my thinking and concentration, I can draw to me certain objects or certain things, or create a certain environment in which I can place myself, with the power of thought.

I'm glad to have spoken, Riblet. Let us say a prayer before we leave:

Father, we recognize ourselves as being one with You. Like children, we lift our eyes, hearts, and thoughts to You. Help us for this little while to realize better and better our at-one-ment with You. We come unto You, and You will give us what we need. Amen.

Good night. This is George speaking.

Later, as Rib listened to the tape, he was elated and full of wonderment. He played it through again and again. While he recognized his voice, he heard deviations from his own style of speaking. Noticing the different inflections, phraseology, and hesitations of his guide's voice, he felt sure this really was another personality—one in contrast to his own. The sight of the red-headed violinist at the concert came to mind, and he chuckled as he wondered what his friends would say if he told them of George's revelation of life on the other side.

chapter 4

A NEW MISSION AND
TROUBLE IN THE HEARTLAND

Exhilarated by his recent experiences, Rib decided to seek out spiritualist groups or churches. He looked for and found an announcement in a Fort Wayne newspaper that promoted services in a spiritualist church, then persuaded his sister to join him in attending a meeting. It turned out to be a turning point in his life.

Greeted by a small congregation in an upper-story room of a downtown Fort Wayne office building, Rib and Helen felt an immediate sense of belonging. They lent their voices to familiar Christian hymns, then were treated to scripture readings and a brief sermon. And as one of the tenets of spiritualism is that people on the earth plane can be in touch, through mediums, with loved ones on the other side, the gathering also included spirit-world messages to various people in attendance.

After taking in and discussing this Sunday evening service, the siblings were happy to have found the group. They returned again and again.

Rib was now encouraged to speak openly about his psychic experiences. Never at a loss for words, he was heartened by the congregation's enthusiastic response to his informal talks and accepted an invitation to present an occasional lecture in place of the usual sermon. Before long, he wondered if perhaps psychic teaching might be his mission, his avocation in life. And with this goal in mind, he visited a spiritualist community near Anderson, Indiana, called Camp Chesterfield.

Less than an hour's drive from Indianapolis, Camp Chesterfield was, as its 1935 brochure stated, "a haven to those seeking psychic development." From its founding, in 1886, as a summer retreat, it had grown continuously and by the mid 1930s had a sizable population of year-round residents. It remains to this day a thriving community, nestled in a peaceful scenic setting. At the time of Rib's initial visit, it consisted of gravel roads, private cottages, two hotels, a cafeteria, a book store, a gift shop, a chapel that served as an auditorium, and a few meditation sites. Entering through a historic stone gate, visitors were greeted by a beautiful, oval-shaped park filled with bushes and flowers. One guest, who had been there in 1935 as well as in recent years, spoke of the beauty and peacefulness of the place, saying it was like "the land that time forgot."

A typical day's roster afforded sessions with mediums, clairvoyants, and crystal-ball readers. Communal activities included séances, healing services, and lectures. When Rib was introduced to the president of the organization, he told her of his psychic work as well as his experience in lecturing at the spiritualist church in Fort Wayne. Soon enough, he became a popular speaker on the podium at Camp Chesterfield.

As they learned that Riblet was a physician, visitors at the camp sought him out for medical treatment and word soon spread that his healing ability seemed out of the ordinary. While it was many years before he was aware of it, his exceptional diagnostic skills were due to his psychic ability. "I thought all physicians could see and know intuitively the cause of the symptoms that patients brought in," he confessed. He was becoming known as a healer.

Although he was kept busy with his frequent trips to Camp Chesterfield during the summers, as well as with the responsibilities of his thriving medical practice in Goshen, Riblet also found time to type up his thoughts and beliefs for future use. His byline appeared in periodicals such as *Rosicrucian Magazine*, the *Dale News*, the *Progressive Thinker*, and the British publication, *The Light*, communicating his belief in life after death and the scientific importance of mediumship. Years later, Robert Crookall, an English out-of-body-experience researcher, came across these articles and quoted Riblet in at least three of his many books.

Still, for all his ease in sharing his psychic experiences at Chesterfield and in print, in his hometown Rib kept the subject of his lectures and writings to himself and a very few close friends. A distressing episode with a local Christian minister exemplifies just how deeply religious bigotry was embedded in Rib's own backyard.

"I became acquainted with a minister who was slightly older than myself," he related of the incident. "I found the man friendly and one afternoon had occasion to chat with him at length, sharing some of my psychic experiences and spiritual beliefs."

Rib later told a friend about his encounter with the minister and the friend cautioned Rib about being too revealing. "You never know who might use such information to your detriment," he warned.

"No," Rib scoffed. "This minister is an open-minded man."

This same friend, a secret practitioner of spiritualism, belonged to a local civic organization and obtained Rib's permission to offer his name for membership. A closed society, and one in which the minister was also a member, the membership had the power to deny applicants admission. When Riblet's name was submitted for a vote, the "open-minded" minister leapt to his feet and objected. "Dr. Hout believes in spirits," he said scornfully. "He's a spiritualist! Such a man is not a suitable candidate for this organization." Had Rib's friend not placed his name in nomination, or witnessed the outburst, Rib would have remained naively unaware of the duplicity of the "friendly" minister who blackballed him.

Soon after, Rib spied his name in a tabloid-type magazine article. The bylined reporter had indeed chatted with Rib, who had meant his remarks as nothing more than a friendly exchange—an off-the-record interview. Now, here, on the rack of a hometown drugstore newsstand, Rib spotted the story headlined in a sensational weekly. The story, while spec-tacular in this small conservative town in the Heartland, would have been an ordinary and accepted account in any gathering of spiritualists. Rib had told the reporter of his see-ing fairies and goblins as a child, of being able to speak to rel-atives and friends who had died, and he revealed one of his out-of-body experiences. He also detailed his first prophecy, as a teenager. It was World War I and Helen, who was away in Fort Wayne in nurse's training, became critically ill during the famous "big flu epidemic." According to her doctor, she was not expected to live. Riblet told his parents that Helen *would* live and get well, and that she should come home. He was right. Within a few days, they were able to take her home where she recovered completely.

Now, faced with the tabloid's exposure of his spiritual abilities, Riblet and two close friends drove to every news-stand in town, purchasing all the offending magazines. The next week he had a bonfire and burned every copy. Rib laughed heartily as he related the story years later, but at the time he was a well-respected, small-town physician who had a lot to lose, and there was no turning back at that point.

But Rib wasn't afraid to expose himself to *some* non-believers. A year or two later, there occurred at Chesterfield an amusing anecdote that Rib loved to tell. "Although my dad had no interest whatsoever in spiritualism," he said, "I got him to go down to the camp one time. In a séance, a spirit came in, calling him by his name, Sol, and asked, 'Don't you remember me?' He said, 'No, I don't know who you are.' She talked on, and the full story came out. Both Dad and the young lady had attended an old-time country dance. She had had a very embarrassing experience while on the dance floor. Because her bustle had not been fastened securely enough, it had become unfastened during one of the dizzying whirls of the dance. She lost it, and they had quite a time finding it! With much laughter from the séance attendees and with some embarrassment, my father admitted this incident as a fact and claimed that he believed in the authenticity of the spirit who was speaking."

Because of the intermingling of visitors between Chesterfield and Lily Dale Assembly in western New York state, Riblet was invited to lecture and teach at Lily Dale, the well-known and long-established—in the late 1930s it was celebrating its sixtieth season—spiritualist gathering place located in Chautauqua County. Like Camp Chesterfield, Lily Dale offered many enticements, with two hotels, guest houses, a large assembly hall for lectures and other presentations, a library, a bookstore, a cafeteria, two cafés, and a gift shop. Guests also enjoyed swimming, boating, and hiking. It was an exciting place, hosting such visitors and lecturers as Mahatma Gandhi, President and Mrs. Franklin Roosevelt, and Sir Arthur Conan Doyle. (More recently, Lily Dale has been host to such guest lecturers as Wayne Dyer, Raymond Moody, Shakti Gawain, and Whitley Strieber.)

Riblet spent five summer seasons at Lily Dale. Known there as a popular teacher and speaker, he was also respected for his healings. Mrs. Hilda Wilkinson, a well-known senior citizen who has lived on the grounds for over fifty years, reported that many people at Lily Dale said, "If you want a *good* healing, go to Riblet Hout." She also commented that whenever he lectured, the hall was filled.

Back home, although busy with his practice, Rib made time to meditate every day. During these sessions, he found peace of mind, answers to problems, and inspiration. Because he was learning more than most people about the workings of the universe and was able to visit friends and relatives on the other side, Riblet looked forward to more astral projections. And his hope was soon fulfilled; the following is his description of an out-of-body experience, as put down in his journal and entitled—

A Spiritual Conference at Camp Chesterfield

This was really an excursion tonight. We did many things and moved rapidly from place to place. Perhaps it was my restless mind, or maybe it was the psychic atmosphere here—anyway we did much in a very short time.

First, I lay down on the bed in the lighted room and bandaged my eyes to help me relax and keep light interference from bothering me. Then I simply breathed a few deep breaths and raised up a little, free from my body.

I was in my ordinary clothes this time in the etheric body, [wearing] duplicates of my physical garments. This seemed strange to me as I usually wear some sort of simple robe, but I soon could see why. George stood there by me in clothes similar to mine and beckoned me to follow him through the closed door of the room and down the long corridor of the hotel.

"Well, well," I remember thinking, "We're surely staying here on earth this time." In a moment we were up in the hotel lobby [of Camp Chesterfield], George and I, in our astral bodies. There sat the people, guests and friends chatting freely with one another. I noted the position of several people, to ask them about it later. I wondered, too, at the time, if any of them would be able to see me.

We tarried here but a short time and then George motioned me to follow him through the closed screen doors. I followed him out of the hotel, across the porch, past many people there, and thence out, down the path, across the park toward the cottages of the mediums, where circles of materialization and direct voice were being held.[1]

It was night, I knew from physical knowledge, but as I was now in my etheric body, things were plainly visible to me, and even the darkness was not apparent. I was moving with George in some mysterious, luminous twilight that was very soft and restful to my etheric vision, and yet all things were plainly visible to me. I noticed that all the buildings and even the trees were softly luminous, much as things appear to the physical eye upon a very bright moonlight night. But tonight I knew I was not in the light of the moon—the sky was cloudy.

We walked on, or rather glided on, until we came to the cottage of a medium I knew well. I was very interested in the many, many spirit entities we met and passed. So many seemed to be going and coming, moving or gliding either silently along or passing us in groups, laughing and talking.

Now my attention was drawn to a light we were approaching. It was as though a huge luminous circle had opened up before us. There sat a group of people in a circle, singing a song. I knew they were in the physical body, seated in a trumpet circle[2] making conditions for a spirit contact. I now stood quietly in the room, in a corner, with George.

We watched the spirit people quietly descend and step over to meet the spirit [in charge] and give him their names and their relationship to particular people present in the room. I watched them melt themselves into the ectoplasmic mass[3] in the center of the room so the vibrations of their voices might be condensed, or "stepped down." This was to affect the physical atmosphere of the room, and thus they might talk to their friends in the physical body.

All was accomplished and carried through in a very businesslike manner. It was an event, from my side of the picture, which I shall never forget, for it showed me the reality of the harmony of the two sides in a direct-voice séance.

Now I felt the call back to the physical body. I knew we must leave the séance, so I mentally acquiesced to that thought. This time it was really no sooner said than done, for I found myself suddenly in my room at the hotel, standing there beside the physical body again. It was breathing quietly and rhythmically, and George said there was no need to hurry this time in getting back, that he could now take me to some activities in the etheric world.

Again, a flash, a sense of rushing, pulling upward, and I found myself in a large circular room, hearing the soft persistent buzz of conversation—words being spoken by many voices.

My etheric vision gradually became used to the new vibration of life upon which I now found myself, and I centered my gaze, with interest, on a group of gentlemen who were talking about "Chesterfield, the Camp," spiritual contacts with the earth plane there, and such. So I shamelessly listened in.

I found this was a group of spiritual directors of the camp. They were trying to arrange newer contacts and better psychic conditions there. I remember clearly now who some of the men were who were talking about the situation. One of them was Thomas Jefferson, another was Thomas Paine, and another was Tom Smith. I knew by the earnestness of the conversation, and the plans I saw they were attempting to follow, that great things in the future were being planned for this place. I was much impressed by the general atmosphere of peace and power in the room.

Now George motioned me to come with him again, and so we left this group. We again appeared to soar upward through space. I received the knowledge in some way that George was taking me to his home. I was very grateful to him for this chance and privilege.

Now we entered an atmosphere of mystic light of the softest blue tint. All of the landscape took on a hue of deep blue and purple, much like the afterglow of the twilight on a clear winter evening, when the soft sunset lights all the snow and landscape with deep, dark, restful purple.

Here we found ourselves just outside George's home, sitting on a small cliff overlooking the deep-purple waters of a quiet mountain lake. George explained that here, now, it was also his nighttime, and that it was always like this for certain periods of his daytime.

I sat quietly, silently, looking out, awestruck with the magnificence of the scene before me. The distant trees, the skyline at the edge of the water, the soft deep-purple flow, the spiritual hush over everything, still is imprinted in my memory as one of those imperishable mental pictures I shall always carry with me. I simply turned to George, in awestruck wonder at it all.

But of course such joy could not last forever. Nothing as perfect as that could be held long, it seemed to me. So I automatically responded to the signal to return to earth . . . A soft blurring sensation, a blotting out of this restful soft purple, a feeling of smothering descent, and here I am again in my physical body.

As he relived the latest encounter with his spirit guide, Rib was deeply affected. This was not what he had learned in Sunday school, and the recent experience with the minister entered his mind, however briefly. As he stared at the words he had written in his little red book, the memory flooded his mind as he relived the adventure. Once again, although torn about his beliefs, he felt an awareness, a knowing in his heart, that what he saw and heard was real. From the many books he had read, he knew he was not alone in having this experience, but he felt a deep need to share this remarkable meeting with another earthbound person.

Two families who had experienced Riblet's healings had become close and were anxious to learn more from their doctor/confidant. By inviting them for an evening of discussion which lasted late into the night, Rib gained their enthusiastic support and their encouragement to be open to further spiritual encounters. He felt very privileged to have been chosen to receive the information but had no idea that this was just the beginning.

The following day, struggling to find the right words and motivated by passion, he recorded his thoughts on the tape recorder. Speaking haltingly and hesitantly at first, Riblet expressed his deep emotional feelings about the existence of both spiritual power and George.

George Is *Real*

I wish I could tell you how I feel about the *real* reality of spiritual power. It's *real*. It's . . . it's . . . just as though . . . it's, uh . . . life; it's . . . uh . . . actual; it's . . . it's . . . it's . . . uh . . . a part of my everyday doing. I feel that I have the power and the ability, and the naturalness of taking . . . this something . . . this energy . . . this vitality, this reality of spirit, and using it as . . . naturally as . . . uh . . . I . . . *breathe*, as I move my hands, as I recognize the things about me. I feel George as an actual entity, real, like, uh, like my good friend Robert is. Why he's so real that he seems just like Robert. He and Robert could talk together. He's here. Oh, it's *good* to feel that it's . . . it's *actual*. It isn't a fantasy, and it isn't something I've dreamed up.

My friends are a part of my life. They intertwine themselves in a way that makes it real and substantial. George is here just as they are. He's *George*, just like Charles is *Charles*. There isn't any difference! He has a physical body in a different way, but it's real. Sometimes I don't even sense the difference of a physical body. I think of him as being like one of my good friends—actual, with a physical body to touch and to help and to treat and to ask about—and utilize the help that he can give me. Oh, golly, George is real.

Anyone may say, "Well, George is a spirit. He isn't here." And to me, that sort of makes me rebel. George *is* here. He has facial expressions, he has curly red hair, he is thin, he manifests uniqueness and individuality. If I would go down the street and see somebody walking in a certain way, holding himself in a certain way, straight and slightly limped, that would seem like George. I would walk up to him and say, "Why, it *is* George." That means he's here. He isn't spirit exclusively. He's physical, shall we say? He draws this physical power from me, he says, and I am the means whereby he can be he, be himself, George on the earth plane, living physically, the only difference being that he is more refined. He doesn't hunger, he doesn't eat pot pie, French fries, or coffee. They aren't necessary—like they are for us.

It seems I can't get along without coffee, and I like so much to go over to Erma's [a small neighborhood restaurant] and have all the coffee I want to drink, and decide what I want—two eggs up, toast and bacon, maybe. I like the atmosphere there, the people who come in, because I feel like I can radiate help to them and enjoy them. Like the man from Freeport, he looks forward to seeing me; and I'm glad to make this contact.

I want Erma to feel better, more alive. George and I'll work on that together. The point I want to make is that George is *real*. He does things his own way. He emphasizes particular things, which is *George*, just like Charles emphasizes particular things, which is *him*—who gets angry over things that don't go right—in a very vociferous manner.

I get up in the morning, and George is here. I go through the day, and George is available for spiritual help, for healing . . .

Oh, golly, it's good to think of George as real and here . . .

[At this point the tape ran out.]

Giving Riblet all manner of information, direction, and help in the many messages he delivered, George observed his protégé, urging him on to fulfill his destiny. In many cases, Rib felt George's presence, receiving an impression about the subject George would be discussing, even before he went into trance. Deciding to follow the advice of his friends, Rib prepared the recorder for preserving whatever his spirit guide wanted to say to him, whenever it seemed appropriate. In the following message, George explains mediumship.

Developing Mediumship

This is George Felbers. I'm very happy to come to you this evening because this is an auspicious time for you whether or not you may recognize it as being so. You are on the threshold of receiving a new type of help from the spirit world, and you will grow with a knowledge of our presence and our help in a way which you have not previously understood.

Through our impressions to you, you have examined and are reading and utilizing the help from Stewart Edward White's book, *The Road I Know*, concerning the mediumship of Betty [White].[4] Betty, who is here with us now and is acquiescing in all that we say, does understand that your approach to mediumship is comparable to her way. She doubted, she hesitated, she questioned, she cooperated when she could conscientiously do so; but she would not acquiesce to the place where she would be subjected to the presence of spirit people. And so it is with you.

We want you to know that our approach to you will be in a cooperative way. You will be a medium, a means, a bridge, a station whereby we can get our thoughts across to you. This will be in a manner very similar to the way Betty "received" when she was able to expand her consciousness. She received through mediumship in the way the "invisibles" [her term for her spirit guides] had taught her.

You also question much, and we have appreciated that. You have gone along well, occasionally, and we have utilized that to a very great degree. Now you are beginning a new phase and a new age, in a new year, in a new manner, so that things will be looking up more than you can comprehend at this time. . . .

Many of the things that you have been doubting and not quite comprehending have come to pass in spite of your doubts. Further, you have been able to fulfill many of the things that we have started out to do. You are much more sensitive, more impressionistic in many ways, and you can receive even without knowledge of our presence. No, we are not making you a subjective medium, wherein we can entrance you involuntarily. You will make conditions so that we can come as you allow us, to be close to you, giving you help from our side, and making you realize that true spiritual power even comes unbidden. As you unfold, accept, realize, and empower yourself with an awareness of our presence, you are consciously expanding your comprehension of the magnitude of spiritual power in such a manner that never again can you come back to hold yourself exclusively to reactions of the earth plane. You cannot be of the earth alone, but you will be dually of the earth and of the spirit world.

Others [in the spirit world] are interested in watching you. In *The Road I Know*, you will read that Betty doubted each step of the way until she could be sure of her invisibles, and you follow in a similar way. We are glad to know that you are accepting, as she accepted, the things which were for you—and the things which we found were for her.

Betty is inspiring you now. She will be with you often, teaching and helping with the phraseology of the words as they come through, making you aware of the helpfulness of interested spirits who are not even a part of your band [group of spirits]. Those of you who are interested in acquiring your own bands of teachers will be given opportunity to accept and to utilize our help. Perhaps in the next sitting that you have with your friends, I will be able to entrance you sufficiently to speak so that they may understand the need of a highly developed spiritual band. These things need to be understood and utilized according to true spiritual law and are for you—and for each of you who are striving toward mediumship or who are looking to communication [between the spirit world and the earth world] as a way of life.

I think that by now you accept the fact that I, George Felbers, am a being apart from you, that there are minds that can work in harmony with yours which are not you and not even a part of your consciousness. I think you can readily see also that there is a power of vibrant energy in the universe, a life force which can be utilized and directed toward those who need your help. You can help the spiritual power. You will be able to direct energy to those patients and friends of yours that need your help. They will be helped knowingly and unknowingly; they will feel the presence of our aid. They will be subject to beginning a new way of life, subjected in that they can hold back or allow the spiritual power to pour into their consciousness, into their bodies, and into their minds in a manner that God's power may follow through much more readily than it does now.

It may seem futile to you—when you stop to consider the tiny little light that you bear in relationship to the magnitude of the universe—that you can touch or are in harmony with the tiny little lights of other millions of people who are on the earth plane and who are also in the spirit world. I know you have questioned the value of the help that you may do, and I know that it will seem insignificant to you, and yet it is not so.

The little bit that we can do to aid you is magnificent in the final sum, and in fact, you and each person about you—each person that you contact—is needed for the upward evolutionary way of spiritual power as a way of life, looking toward God. You know, God needs each of you. Each little point of light is an individual point of light. You don't stop to think often enough that you, as an individual, are unique, as are all other individuals about you. No one else is like you. No one else can take another's place.

You definitely have a part to play. When you renege, withhold, doubt, question, or hold back, you are thwarting, temporarily, the rush of spiritual power. It may seem insignificant to you, but it is not so. Taken as a whole, your way of life is important. The spiritual ideas you foster are helpful not only to yourself, but to others about you. How else can life progress without the help of those who aid in progression?

Surely, the life force, or energy, or will power cannot be cast out willy-nilly and assume a certain path, a certain manner, or a certain way of expressing itself. It needs direction, and it needs help; it needs amplification of power which you alone can give. You and your friends are distinct and individual, needed and wanted. You are *you*! And no person can live your life for you, with you, apart from you, or about you. You are *you*, and your friends are *themselves*. They're very valuable to us, and you are, too. We are hoping that you understand that we are very valuable to you, too. We wish our way not to be an empty way from your viewpoint. We wish it to be a way of looking up, going beyond, and expanding into the higher godhood which is your true heritage.

You can, with your natural psychic powers, expand your life in such a way that it will touch other lives. More and more and more lives will be touched until this great wave of spiritual power will be broadened. And when the true Aquarian Age is at hand (and you are in the foreshadowing of it now), then life will be simpler. Complex problems will fade away. The doubts and fears and hesitations will be things of the past.

We're grateful and thankful that we, on the spirit side, can come to you to aid and bless you. We can administer and utilize your help in a way that would not be possible except that you allow us, working in harmony with us and showing us your wish to progress.

I would just like to breathe a little prayer to you before I leave. I want you to know that we are spiritually aware of God's great universal radiation of energy, that we are a part of God and His power, and we look up to Him as the Light of light and the Crown of crowns and the Help of help. We look backward to your plane of life, a physical plane, and we say that we can amplify your spiritual prayers and your aspirations and your will to give of yourself for others. We are humbly grateful that we are instruments of God's power for the magnification of spiritual light, just as you and your friends are vehicles and powers. You are our instruments for good, as we are instruments of God for good; and together, we are going to amplify and strengthen and guide the spiritual power and light until it has a brilliance and a reality which you can comprehend even now.

The way is open for you, and you are doing well. You are receiving daily, more and more consciously, an appreciation of our presence with you. We are never beyond the power of thought to come to you. As you call, we will come.

Now we have gathered ourselves into a circle of divine power. We are radiating that power on to you. You are receiving a bond in mind and spirit. Our blessings go with you; they fill you with dynamic energy. They radiate spiritual power. They are for you, a god in the making, and you can open yourself to receive.

Father, we thank Thee for these things which *are*. We ask that we will, all together, knowingly, understand Thy way; and that we can conscientiously say with You, Give us this day our daily bread and forgive us our trespasses, and our minds will not lead us into temptation as we go, but will give us greater power and understanding and blessings and help forever and ever. Amen.

George speaking. Good night, Riblet. It's so good to have been here with you. Again, good night.

Though feeling somewhat soothed and supported by George's message, Riblet was still unable to accept, without hesitation, all that had been revealed to him. It would take further messages, further experiences, to eliminate fully Rib's doubts. Fortunately, both were on their way to him.

chapter 5

AN EXTRAORDINARY
MYSTICAL EXPERIENCE

At the age of thirty, Riblet was living and working as a physician in Goshen, Indiana. His aunt Ada lived about a half hour's drive away, in Middlebury, where Riblet had been born and raised. My mother lived in another city, but she was present to care for the aunt, Ada Riblet Strome, who was critically ill.

Rib drove to his aunt's home in the early evening of May 5, 1933. While his visit was professional, it was also very personal. The last surviving member of his mother's family, Aunt Ada had helped to raise him. Now seventy-three, she had recently been confined to bed with cancer of the stomach. And although it was assumed her illness was terminal, there was no reason to believe death was imminent.

But she did die. And in an article that was eventually published in England in 1935,[1] Rib described the event in detail:

Resurrection!
Doctor Witnesses Liberation of Dying Woman's Spirit Body

As a prelude to the relating of this experience, I wish to say that I am not a professional medium, and I have not, as yet, publicly acclaimed my interest in this work. I am interested in this great truth of active life beyond the grave because of my personal experiences and because I see in it a scientific fact that has not been successfully refuted by material science.

May I add, also, that prior to this earnest watching of the spirit body leaving the material one, I had not read or been able to find any facts similar to that which I witnessed. I had not read of the actual process of the soul leaving the body, and I had not known of the cord that connects the spirit body with the earth body.

So what I saw could not have been a dramatization of the subconscious in a moment of emotional stress, for all this was beyond the knowledge of either my conscious or sub-conscious mind.

With this brief foreword, may I relate this experience of watching the withdrawal of the spirit body from the physical counterpart and the gradual formation of the astral body immediately above the physical vehicle.

Process of Dying

Perhaps this experience which I relate is unique in that the transition was very slowly brought about. In fact, the actual process of "dying" covered almost twelve hours, a period of time from seven in the evening until seven the next morning. And all through these long night hours, I, with members of my family, sat at the bedside of an only aunt and watched the phenomenon of physical life gradually cease and ebb away.

But I, personally, saw much more than this. I saw physical death on one plane and a birth of life into another. In other words, I saw the withdrawal of the spirit body from the physical body and its re-formation and reintegration immediately above the physical body, suspended about two feet in midair above the death bed.

I called quite early in the evening at the home of my aunt, who lived in a neighboring small town near my home. While I had been caring for her professionally, my interest in her was much greater than professional, for she was the last surviving member of my mother's family and one who had always been much like a mother to me.

This evening I had gone to see her from a sense of love and duty and to see that she was made as comfortable as possible. She was seventy-three years old, had been surprisingly young and active all her life, and had only been bedfast for the last ten days. A previous diagnosis of gastric carcinoma had been made and, while we knew that recovery was impossible, we did not look for an immediate demise. So I called, this evening of her transition, not even surmising that the change would come so soon.

The Silver Cord
As I watched the suspended spirit body, my attention was called, again intuitively, to a silver-like substance that was

streaming from the head of the physical body to the head of the spirit double. Then I saw the connecting cord between the two bodies. As I watched, the thought, "The Silver Cord," kept running through my mind. I knew, for the first time, the meaning of it. This Silver Cord was the connecting link between the physical and the spirit bodies, even as the umbilical cord unites the child to its mother.

I noticed especially, then, this cord and its attachments. I saw that it was fastened and attached to each of the bodies at the occipital protuberance, immediately at the base of the skull. I could even see the way the cord was attached—just where it met the physical body, it spread out, fan-like, and numerous little strands separated and attached separately to the skull base. Other than at the attachments, the cord was round, being perhaps about an inch in diameter. The color was a translucent, luminous silver radiance. The cord seemed alive with vibrant energy. I could see pulsation of light stream along the course of it, from the direction of the physical body to the spirit double. When the pulsation would start at the base of the physical brain, the glow would follow through until it swelled into light at the other extreme of the cord. And with each pulsation, the spirit body became more alive and denser, whereas in contrast the physical body became quieter and more nearly lifeless.

All of the above phenomena took place during the long hours of the night. During this time there was spirit activity extraneous to the spirit's metamorphosis.

Spirit Presences Around the Bed

I was aware of spirit presences in the room. I heard soft chanting, as though many voices were softly singing, but I could not then distinguish any words. I glanced up, away from the bed, and looked into the faces of those loved ones of our family who had previously passed away from the physical through death.

My uncle, the deceased husband of my aunt, stood there beside the bed. Also, her son, passed away many years previously, stood silently watching the birth and death. Also three other aunts, sisters, stood beside me. And then, as though I felt, rather than saw her, I looked up into the living, animated face of my own mother, who had passed on about five years before.

We were all there together—those from our side of life to witness the death of this beloved one, and those from the other side to welcome her arrival into a new place of life. Thus we watched the long night through. During the course of the night, I witnessed several other interesting phenomena. At one time, as I was watching the white coverlet on the bed, my attention was called to something above the spirit body. I looked toward the ceiling of the room, and there floated down upon the bed a veritable shower of deep-red rose petals! These seemed to fall so thick and heavy that to my spiritual vision the white bedspread was entirely obliterated. In its place was a covering of soft deep-red rose petals. I sensed the symbology that the "bed of death" was really a "bed of birth," and the deep red symbolized the beginning of a healthy new life.

A little later my attention was called to the head of the high, old-fashioned bed in which my aunt lay. There I saw placed upon the bedstead, by spirit hands, an exquisite wreath of deep-red roses—again the symbol of a life almost completely finished on earth.

As the spirit friends and loved ones were gathering, I noted with interest (and commented to family members present) that my sister was able to distinguish variously colored pinpoints of light placed about the room at the places where I saw members of the spirit group. The actual placing of the lights where I saw members of the spirits was an interesting corroboration. Among the spirit friends gathered were Ada's son and her husband.

As the dawn of the new day approached, I became aware that the final passing could not be much longer delayed. Physical signs of cessation of life were apparent, and I communicated this knowledge to the waiting family.

Then again I watched the formation of the spirit body. By this time the duplicate of the physical form was striking indeed. The spirit draperies had been softly folded about the quiet spirit form. The features were very clear and distinct, and an attitude of serene repose was upon the countenance. The greatest contrast that was presented to me between the two bodies was the difference between maturity and old age, of life and death. For now the animation and life was all in the astral body, and the physical had entirely stopped the restless moving, was entirely oblivious to all reflexes, and death seemed imminent. The pulsation of the cord had stopped. It was less luminous and was shrunken. But the attachments were still complete.

Even as I looked at it, I was astonished to hear an external voice softly whisper in my ear, "Only twelve minutes more!" I communicated this to the family and sat expectantly waiting, watch in hand. I watched the cord at its point of emergence from the physical body. I looked at the various strands of the cord as they spread out, fan-like, at the base of the skull. I saw the strands sever and snap, one at a time. Each strand snapped and curled back as would a taut wire if it was suddenly cut. I saw these strands snap one by one until only one strand connected the cord to the body. I glanced at my watch. The twelve minutes had gone by!

Final Liberation

The final severance was at hand. A twin process of death and birth was about to ensue. I watched expectantly and anxiously. By spiritual vision I saw, symbolically I am sure, a pair of golden shears. These shears opened and closed. The last connecting strand of the Silver Cord snapped, and the spirit body was free! This spirit body, which had been supine before, now rose and stood upright behind the bed, where it paused momentarily before commencing its upward flight from the room. As I looked at this radiant, luminous apparition, the closed eyes opened and a smile broke upon the radiant features. Animation was there. A newly awakened life looked at me with a nod of recognition. Then she gave me a smile of farewell. Then this spirit form vanished from my sight. She looked the same as she had before death, but now a vibrant, vital, younger person smiled at me; she was a person in her prime and not one who could possibly be seventy-three years old.

The above phenomena were witnessed by me as an entirely objective reality. The spirit forms I saw with the aid of my physical eyes. The voices I heard were spoken as one human would speak to another. This did not occur to me as a fleeting vision, which would come and go with startling swiftness. The whole of this event covered twelve hours. I watched, commented, and moved about during the occurrence. One other person in the room was aware of other than physical forces; and, comparing notes later, we brought out veritable inferences.

Since the above was witnessed, other contacts have been made whereby I have conversed with and seen other spirit folk. But never has this experience been repeated, nor has such objective phenomena occurred which has covered as long a period of time.

But I am absolutely certain that contacts with the "next place of existence" can frequently be made, and that the contact can be a perfectly natural and normal occurrence.

Later, my mother spoke about her own experience on the night of Aunt Ada's death. Mother had had two years of nurse's training, so was experienced in the sick room. "It was very interesting," she said. "You know, I insist that we choose the time to die. Ada had been having so much pain and was rather restless. She would have to get up to use the commode, and I was helping her, but she didn't say anything.

Rib came in right after he was through work and checked her and gave her some medication. When she was settled down and seemed to be comfortable, we took the few steps to the kitchen and had something to eat. We started writing cards to the relatives, so that they'd all know her condition.

"I had the impulse to go in to see how she was, and she was dying. I went out to Rib and I said, 'Aunt Ada is dying!' He didn't believe it because he knew she had been all right a few minutes beforehand. I said, 'Nevertheless, she's dying.' I could tell by her pulse."

After checking his aunt again, Riblet went back into the kitchen and said "Well, she certainly is." Their step-grandmother Riblet lived only a few blocks away, and Riblet left to bring her to the bedside.

My mother corroborated her brother's extraordinary experience during the passage of their aunt. "He told us about what he was seeing," she said, "the spirit form and all of that. He said he had never seen anything like this before. None of us had. He first said there was something like a cloud over her body, and then as she lay there, at one period, he saw a big basket or bushel of roses dropped down on her. I didn't see this, but I knew there was something. I saw the cloud.

"We all sat there, as her breathing gradually got shorter and shorter. She was in a coma. Grandma was crying—they were very close. It took twelve hours."

Finally, my mother pointed out that although Aunt Ada had suffered all day, as soon as Riblet got there, the transition commenced. "She evidently didn't want me to be alone," my mother explained. "I would have been alone with her."

After sharing this experience in more detail with his sister, Rib expressed the thought that, in a sense, Aunt Ada was healed from her dreadful disease. "You, know," he said, "within only twelve hours, that dear soul went from a bed of pain to a live, robust, younger, smiling self!"

My mother added, "If everyone who's grieving for a loved one could be aware of what happens when we die, perhaps they could work through their grief quicker and more easily."

Up to this point, although others had spoken of his healing capabilities, Riblet had never actually thought of himself as a healer. The experience inevitably led him to thoughts of some of his patients and how he had helped them. He was to learn much more on this subject.

chapter 6

THE ASTONISHED HEALER

As an osteopath, Riblet was not trained in prescribing medications—at least not in the early years. He mainly depended upon osteopathic manipulations to heal his patients, and he was pleased with the positive results he achieved with these treatments. He couldn't explain how the laying on of hands could heal; he just accepted it and assumed all doctors worked in the same way—healing with touch, diagnosing through intuition.

His practice grew steadily, despite the fact that he was away from home from time to time, attending to his spiritual work of lecturing, teaching, and conducting séances. But he never had to make an announcement to his patients upon his return home, since calls for appointments began almost as soon as he got back. His office was in his home, and his patients simply watched for his car to determine when he would be available.

Intuitively, he began to recognize the presence of George, and sometimes other entities, while attending to his patients, and he sought the truth about the aid of spirit helpers, deciding to ask his guide for this information. He lay on his bed with the tape recorder at hand, and received answers to his questions.

George's Message on Healing

RIBLET: I feel George around me, and I'm requesting that he tell me about the possible help I sometimes receive from the other side in treating my patients. It's not always apparent, and I wonder if I can do anything to improve my techniques or treatments?

GEORGE: Dear Riblet, I am happy to speak to your question.

In your healing, you have greater power than you can comprehend. You will have patients that respond magnificently, just simply to the laying on of hands, which is very good. You will have patients who will not respond because of their thinking, because of karmic reaction, because of laws of cause and effect, or because of spiritual static—or, rather, physical static in a spiritual world. That should not deter you. You should go on with each patient, hoping, praying, aligning yourself with spiritual power, doing the best you can, knowing that the invisible potential of each patient is there in perfection, and all you must do is bring it out.

When you attend a patient, know that it is a serious matter. You are surrounded by beings who can be helpful whenever the patient comes in for a treatment. It's the same as when a surgeon enters an operating room and everything and everybody needed are in place to assist him. So it is with a spiritual treatment, and also physical osteopathic treatments. Power is at work. It is manifesting, changing molecular activity, and changing the metabolism of the body. It is changing the relationship of body, soul, and mind. It is bringing about changes whereby that person, upon whom you are concentrating your energy, will be able to do more to expand his spiritual reality, which will give him great help and credit when he comes over here. Because he may scoff at the things you are doing and thinking, it is wise to keep them quiet and unobtrusive. Yet these things are just as real as a drink of water or a word spoken.

You have a great, wonderful teacher/master here—Adair. He is aiding and healing and giving you advice about things to do, and with that he is perfectly capable of manipulating spiritual substance in a way that can be favorable for your onward progress spiritually. In spiritual healing, he works with vibrations of nature and spiritual force and universal harmony. He can call out the negative aspects of the cells of the physical body, and replace them with positive forces of love, spiritual truth, and of good—making all things right. Adair is able to step up time, as it were, to shorten the duration of cause and effect, to bring the effect much closer to the cause, without so much time in between.

You know how it is in medicine, and in any form of healing, such as with a cut or a bad wound. The doctors give antibiotics, they sterilize the field, and they place sutures so that healing can take place more rapidly. They may bring about conditions whereby healing can be assured, but all this takes time. Nature takes time to heal the wound, but nature does it. With Adair, help will be at hand to promote healing much, much quicker.

With spiritual aspirations, with prayer, with the power of God working for you, through longing and effort and meditation, you can work with us over here, doing infinitely more than you could do alone. It is not your power, my power, or the power of Adair, although his power is greater than you can comprehend. It is tremendous. But the power stems directly from God and no other. God has several different aspects, but the aspect of energy, of power, of ongoing force is probably one of His greatest assets.

You are God's helper. You are a chosen instrument— through earlier lifetimes—whereby you can function both in my world and yours, too. That's what this is all about. That is why you were born and find yourself right where you are now.

It may seem uncanny, unfathomable to you. Adair is a specialist at manipulating spiritual healing power. He can make himself agreeable to the forces and the laws of life that allow him to use this healing force in accomplishing seeming miracles. They are not miracles, of course. It is simply natural law applied in a divine manner, the way of life that shortens the duration of cause and effect. It is primarily here and now.

We can help you in your clairvoyance and your clairaudience.[1] We can bring [spirit] people to you; we can hold others back who would come; and we can make better the communication and the contacts with my world. Remember the threshold toward spirit awareness is a very subtle factor. It isn't a hard and fast thing, and it is changeable—but it *is* reality.

In the times when you hesitate, doubt, wonder, and disbelieve—and there will be some—just know that we are silently standing by, never letting you be alone. You're a part of a spiritual band. You should never have loneliness, because others are always with you.

This is George speaking. Good night, Riblet.

Rib rarely remembered what was said on the tapes at the time George was speaking. Listening to this recording, Rib heard things that he had never learned from his extensive library on spiritual matters. The notion that there was a "being" helping him—Adair—whose specialty was healing, was mind boggling! And the idea that his treatments could help his patients in their spiritual lives, without it even being talked about, was even more amazing to him. Though thankful to have this information, Rib found it hard to think of himself as other than an everyday doctor, let alone one through whom powerful, divine, healing forces flowed. But he had to admit that there were numerous patients who experienced almost magical cures when, in some cases, Riblet had barely touched them.

Riblet's healings were subtle, without ceremony. While his patients often said, "He didn't do anything," or "He just touched the place where I was in pain," they were frequently cured of their afflictions—sometimes after a course of treatments, and sometimes at the first visit. In some cases, he pointed to the painful spots before the patient told him where they were. So it is strange that Rib was often heard to say that it was many years before he actually realized he was a healer. "I thought all osteopaths had the same results that I did," he staunchly declared. "I thought *that was* osteopathy!"

Patients often made comments about the strength and energy of the doctor's hands. Once when Riblet had placed his hands on a patient's back, he left behind red hand prints. Even at Riblet's funeral, the minister repeated several times, "Those healing hands."

Through taped interviews with patients, accounts by Riblet and his friend Charles, and through my own direct conversations with some of Riblet's patients, I have come to know of numerous healings Rib performed. And many of the patient's histories follow the same pattern. The following few accounts are typical of those that I've learned of over the years, and each illustrates the practical results of George's theories regarding healing—and Riblet's abilities in particular:

As the result of an accident years earlier, William Cleary suffered with a pinched sciatic nerve and had been taking medication regularly to help relieve his back pain. In addition, his work as a draftsman required that he lean forward much of the time, and this contributed to his problem. Because there was a fifty/fifty chance he would not survive an operation, an orthopedic surgeon had told him that surgery could not be attempted. William finally went to Riblet and, feeling so much better after the first visit, he returned regularly for a number of years. The grateful patient described what he experienced during a treatment. He felt the heat from Riblet's hands when they were several inches away. "I felt as if the hand was inside when Dr. Hout treated my back," he said, "and I felt a glow inside afterward. The muscles that were knotted from spasm just relaxed and relieved that terrible pain."

Riblet said that William could easily have ended up in a wheelchair, but in fact had been able to continue working, with little or no pain.

When Riblet helped Diana Peterson's young daughter, Denise, without either osteopathic manipulation or other orthodox medical procedure, she was much impressed with the results. "When my daughter was an infant," Diana said, "she suffered from a terrible cough as soon as she was put down in her bed. We rarely, if ever, got a full night's sleep. Because our family doctor was never able to find the source of the problem, I was becoming frantic—one time the baby just couldn't seem to catch her breath. After a friend suggested an osteopath, I made an appointment with Dr. Hout.

"Denise was so tiny on that big treatment table, but he just played with her and talked to her, then put his hand on the back of her neck. I took her home, and that evening we got the first full night's sleep we had gotten in months. She slept the whole night through—no coughing or anything. It really impressed me. And the most memorable thing was that the doctor didn't seem to do anything! Although I took her in for a few more treatments in the following months, there was such a great improvement, that, after her recovery, the problem never reappeared."

Thomas Grant had suffered with sciatica for years and hadn't been able to sleep in his bed for eighteen months. He was in agony. Again, Riblet claims, "I really didn't do anything except put my hands on his sore spots, and told him to come in the next day. He went home and was able to sleep in his bed that night, and ever after. He got over his problem entirely."

In fact, Mr. Grant got more excited about the "cure" than the doctor did; he was irritated because Rib, he said, "didn't do anything"!

James had been the victim of a serious railroad accident. After undergoing two spinal operations, he was discharged from the hospital. Having an appointment with Riblet, he walked in using crutches. The doctor ran his hand down the spine and pointed out spots that were causing pain. James took treatments twice a week for six weeks, discarded the crutches after the second treatment, and enjoyed a complete recovery. He too spoke about the heat from Riblet's hands when he had a treatment. He also had stomach symptoms, which abated with the doctor's touch. His wife, Beatrice, said James thought "Doc" could heal anything.

Later, James and the family were building a garage. As Beatrice explained: "James kept saying, 'We have to hurry, we have to hurry,' but I would have preferred to take it a little easier. We finished it in October, and he had a severe stroke in December! He was aware even before he had the stroke that his time left was short. Because, in talks with Riblet, he had learned what to expect; he was at peace and was prepared to die. Although he lived for just a few months, James felt he knew what the other side was like, that he would continue on, going forward to a new experience. He read a great deal, but, if it hadn't been for that counseling, he wouldn't have been so well prepared, at ease about dying."

Riblet himself told of an experience that occurred early in his professional life and presented a psychological and emotional healing, rather than a physical one:

I was called in to see a patient who was an inmate in the county jail shortly after I started practice. The doctors in town would take turns in being "on call," and that's how I happened to be there. I was called as a physician, but I was young and ignorant and scared to death.

This young man was an inmate because he had threatened his whole family with guns—he wanted to shoot all of them—and the officials asked me if I would come in and treat him. I was ushered into his padded cell, the door clanked shut, and I was frightened. As I stood there I became aware there was a spirit in the room with us, and I just knew intuitively this was a cousin of the patient, and I said to the boy, "Did you have a cousin who died recently who was awfully interested in guns?"

He said, "Why, yes, I did. How do you know that? John liked his guns and has given them to me, and I want to use them, too."

Then I replied, "Don't you know that your cousin has died, and he isn't interested in guns any more? If I were you, I wouldn't be interested in them either. Why don't you just forget about your cousin, live your life with your parents and enjoy the things you did before?"

He answered, "Well, that would be a good thing." I saw him several more times, and within two weeks, we got him released, and there was no more trouble.

And I myself was once treated by Riblet. I was ten years old and quite ill with rheumatic fever. I lay in bed with pain in every joint—every move I made was agony. Rib made house calls every other day, giving me treatments for over a week until I began to recover. Since penicillin didn't exist at the time, many patients who had even a minor case of this disease were commonly left with a heart murmur. At eighteen and starting my first job, I reported to Rib that because of my health history, the company doctor had examined me at length for life-insurance purposes. "The doctor told me that I had no problem at all with my heart," I told Rib, "and I got the insurance."

In addition to Riblet's healing abilities, what also seems apparent from his patients' accounts is that they were all trusting of the healer, and open to the possibility that healing could occur through means other than traditional medicine. In other words, the patient and the doctor were working in concert, just as George suggested in his message.

Since none of Riblet's patient records were saved, no one will ever know exactly how many patients he helped or cured. There's no question, however, that he changed many lives for the better. As Diana Peterson's daughter Denise once said to Riblet, "Next to Jesus, I love you best!"

But, can the healer heal himself? Rib was middle-aged when he himself was a hospital patient seriously ill with pancreatitis. He had undergone reconstructive surgery of his stomach, had lost a lot of weight, and was unable to take anything by mouth. Although he had been incapable of convincing his doctor to discontinue it, he was being given a certain medication by injection that he intuitively knew was poisoning his system. He suddenly realized that if he didn't eat within two or three days, he would die.

When the surgeon came into Riblet's room, Riblet begged him to stop the drug, telling him bluntly that he would die if it wasn't discontinued. As he explained:

The surgeon stopped, and he studied. He was quiet for fifteen minutes; there wasn't a sound in the room. Finally, without a word, he got up, took the IV out, and said, "Get up."

I'm sure that factor was the turning point in my life. After I had moved around a bit and was back in bed, the reaction came in, and I just felt like there was no more fight left. I thought, "Why go on with this?" There was the awful reaction I was getting from this medicine. My face was very hot, and I was so very thirsty. I was dying of thirst, and I thought, "Why bother?"

My only thought was, "I'll just crawl into a little nest and let nature take its course." I remember floating back into a cave-like place. There were rocks above me and rocks below me, and it seems I may have been lying in water, and yet it was in space. I thought, "Well, let me go." And, all at once, I could see a very big point of light, and that light kept getting bigger and bigger, and glowing brighter and brighter, and kept getting more and more golden, until it just enveloped and surrounded and pulled me—just literally (I could feel that pull). It took my body out of that cave!

After that, I could really feel life in my body. And the light was there. Within a few days I was much better.

What impressed me so was the fact that we've always heard that we hang onto life so resolutely. Well, I recall so distinctly saying to myself, "I'm not hanging onto life; I don't want life, and I want to go, and I don't want to stay here." I wasn't hanging onto it. Life came to me. Now I can truthfully say that life comes and fills us, we don't fill life. I *know* the Power of life is both *outside* and *inside* oneself, and this outside Power can take hold when our personal energy or *will,* or both, fails us. It's a consolation for me to know this. It was the most amazing thing. I remember that, more than anything else of my hospital experience! There was no verbal communication; it was just that pull. I got the message—that it simply was not yet my time. I knew that life was coming to me to keep me here. That I knew, and I knew that I wasn't trying to keep *it.* This was one time I was very sure that I didn't want what I was getting!

Rib regained his strength and was able eventually to resume his practice. And because he felt strongly that we have a certain time to die, as he recuperated he gave much thought to his near-death experience. He wondered why he was meant to remain on this side, and for how long. He lived for a number of years after his encounter with the Light, learning many more lessons from George, including important information about reincarnation.

He also learned about a pact that he had made with George before he was born. And more important, perhaps, he learned why George, in his previous lifetime, had died in his youth.

chapter 7

REINCARNATION AND THE PACT

Having read about reincarnation over the years, Riblet was familiar with the subject. He found that most of the people he met in the spiritualist communities felt this was a reasonable and acceptable belief. Since, to many adults, experience is a teacher unmatched by any other system, living more than one lifetime seemed to make sense—that as one progresses through many lifetimes, both male and female, perhaps with different ethnic origins, he or she naturally becomes a better balanced, more spiritual human being.

After having an out-of-body experience along these lines, Rib felt strongly that reincarnation was indeed a truth. He named this out-of-body experience—

A Former Important Lifetime

At home in my study. Another amazing psychic experience, only this time it was entirely different than ever before. And

grander, too, if that's possible, for I was shown a former important, outstanding embodiment, the last one before this, I believe.

I am a young man named Alvarez. The period is late Inca,
I think. But I must verify this later. I seemed to have attained
near perfection, possessing almost miraculous powers. I was
about six foot, three inches tall, with blue eyes, light brown,
wavy hair that hung to my shoulders. I was dressed in a short
tunic of a soft, cream-colored woolen material that reached to
my knees. This was covered by a breast plate of changeable
deep purple and wine-colored material that looked like velvet.
This glowed with a deep ultraviolet radiance. Around the edge
of this was set a deep-red band that was decorated at intervals
with precious stones: rubies, emeralds, diamonds, and sap-
phires. These glowed with a strange force. Around my head
was a plain gold band studded with similar stones, with a big
white diamond in the center.

The first scene that I saw of myself was when I was walking through the desert. I was walking ahead of several companions when a poisonous snake crept up beside me and was
about to strike. A glance from me and a thrust of my hand sent
a force out which killed the snake. I saw it curl up, turn over,
and die at my feet. This incident took place as we were on our
way to a certain temple to worship.

We went on to the temple which was perfect in its beauty.
It was made entirely of gold and was formed of pillars melted and
blended together in a way similar to our modern buildings . . .

In the temple the group and I advanced to a master who
was seated before us on a throne of gold. He was dynamic and

regal in his poise and power. He was dressed in a simple tunic, as was I, and wore as a token of his power a royal robe of luminous, purple metallic cloth lined with gold. Each of these colors cast a glow on our faces. This teacher's face was staunch and yet very kindly. He wore a short gray beard and had piercing blue eyes.

As we advanced toward him he motioned me to come forward. So I came up in front of him and held out my hand. This was a final initiation ritual which would show him the power I had earned in my attainment. If I won in the demonstration of god power it meant the culmination of this life and the chance to be free to return in some later epoch to the earth to teach others the power I had earned.

So I held out my hands, empty, to him. In them there appeared white hot coals which blazed and burned—but they did not affect me a bit. I heard a murmur from the friends in back of me. Then, suddenly, out of the atmosphere, a dazzling blaze of light struck me just at the base of the brain. I had attained! I was freed from that embodiment for further work in the higher spheres, later to return to earth to teach this knowledge.

I know some of those people who were with me that day. As my immediate personal teacher and instructor I saw the one known as Prince Abjah. He had received his supernormal knowledge from one whom I have known as Cyrius. The one who walked at my side mostly and aided me in my ministry and rituals and worship was George. With him also was Bert Springer, Ben and Betsy Hanson, Bernie Christian, and Charles [friends from Riblet's earth life].[1] All of these especially had a part in my life then; just what relation, I have not yet found out. But I know it will be revealed to me. Robert was also represented as another person and I know not yet who he was. But I will sometime soon receive this information, I know.

My name was Alvarez and my mastership was obtained through Ishtar.

George told me, "This is all I may tell you now."

Rib was quite impressed with this out-of-body experience, for several reasons. While seeing himself in a different lifetime was breathtaking, the fact that his companions were also friends in this lifetime felt strange. Although he had read and heard about others who had out-of-body experiences, he couldn't help but wonder how many had had such an experience. He still just couldn't fully accept that his role in this life was anything more than a small-town physician living an everyday life. After all, he had to pick up his cleaning, wash the dishes, walk the dog, buy groceries, look after his car, and all the rest. He wasn't close friends with any of the other psychics he knew, so he couldn't compare notes. He shared some of his experiences with my mother, but while she was very interested and supportive, she lived in another town and was busy raising me and my siblings. He did have close friends who were interested, but they couldn't share the emotional impact that the unusual encounters had on Rib. He sometimes felt alone and lonesome. So, sometime later, when he felt George around him, he got out his recorder, went into a trance, and waited for a message—

The Prior Pact

RIBLET: I would like to have George come to me and give me his impressions about the work we're doing and anything he would have to say regarding the future of our work and how it may be brought about. I hope he'll have something to say regarding ourselves and our philosophic approach to life and what we may do about it. I'll wait quietly now.

GEORGE: Hello! This is George. I'm very glad to speak. . . .

Remember the *pact* that we'd made previously? Remember the things we said that we would be trying to do through a lifetime on earth? Also, we said that some things we'll do after you come over here. Those things that we have talked about, classified as being important, still are important—first class. Let's make spiritual comprehension the dynamic force of our existence. And let us realize that we, as spiritual beings, together can push back the curtain of ignorance just a bit, helping to expel the darkness from the lives of some people on earth. We can aid, in whatever way, spreading just a bit of spiritual enlightenment on the earth plane.

I don't mean to say that we have the right way exclusively, but that the things that you're doing and the way that we are approaching life and death is a way that follows natural law. It is the way that God wills. It is a way that will give us a great deal of encouragement and enlightenment in the times to come.

You should know that the things that are for you have been predestined. That is to say, you actually applied for the place where you now are living on the earth plane and for the things that you were to do. Before you came onto the physical plane this time, you chose to make conditions whereby certain information would be accessed by you, for giving out to others. In other words, we were reestablishing a contact on the earth plane once more where we might give forth our ideas to help destiny a bit with a group [of spirit entities] that we have worked with in the past.

Things you are doing at this time were planned long before you came into the physical world, and the things that are for you were at hand even before you incarnated as Riblet Hout. So that I could work with you now, things took place which guided my coming onto the earth plane as George Felbers, but leaving very young—in my twenty-third year. This was so I might make manifest to you, here on the earth plane, certain information and certain comprehensions that you would lack memory of, in your present physical incarnation.

I'm glad that you realize the fact that you are a spirit-being, here and now, always will be, and always have been in the past. Occasionally you work with a physical body, but many times you work only with your true etheric body which is yours to have through command, through the ages, and through lives yet to come.

We are attempting to guide your life and your path now, so that soon we can bring into fruition those things which you came to the earth plane to do, just at this time and in this particular body. We have led you to receive the information that is

Above: The house in which Riblet was raised, Middlebury Indiana; *left*, Riblet's sister Helen Hout (later Stein), 9, and Riblet, 5, 1907.

Riblet's father (Solomon "Sol" Hout), sister Helen, and mother (Cora Hout), around 1928.

Above, three generations: Riblet's grandmother, Adeline Riblet, with Helen and Cora, in the 1920s; *below*, Riblet's beloved grandfather, John P. K. Riblet, around 1885.

Above left and right, Riblet
during his high school
years; *below*, in his thirties.

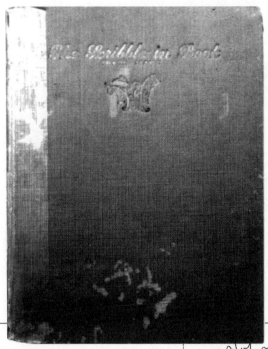

Now faded and
held together
with tape,
"The Scribble in
Book," in which
Riblet recorded
his out-of-body
experiences;
below, a hand-
written page
from the book.

Above, Riblet, on the right, with life-long friend Charles Brennan and Helen, 1969; *below left*, Riblet, in his 60s; *right*, on an island in Michigan where he often went for vacation and retreat, in his 50s.

necessary for you to know or to relearn in order to carry on your work through bringing you books and ideas and thoughts pertaining to our world.

Have you ever stopped to think that each person born on the physical plane is on a path that he started to tread perhaps many millenniums ago, many lifetimes before this? Or it may be that his advent into the earth plane is of fairly recent origin. Anyway, you and I have traveled this way before. We've looked forward and back. We've suffered and we've rejoiced. We have witnessed and we have wept. We have laughed and we have seen the darker things that make up life experiences. But altogether, the way has been a way toward the mountaintop. It's our way of life, and the way we have been traveling has been, I think, an enlightened way.

This has not been given to many people to see. Because of that, we should give of ourselves for the help of those who are looking forward, but haven't yet climbed high enough to see the sunrise of a new day, or to envision life going on and on and on and never stopping. I am glad to know that those on the earth plane who are surrounding you now will accept some of the teachings that we have to give which will be helpful to you and to those who are close to you.

I'd like to have you know that the way you are treading now is the way that you were destined to walk before you entered the earth plane. You have found your way, you have stumbled along, trying in many ways to live up to the pattern, as you intuitively knew it to be. There were other times you deliberately turned your back on the plan of your destined path because you chose to do so. God's law gives you *free will* to do that which you choose to do insofar as your life expression is concerned.

We over here who are working with you must sit by patiently and allow you to express yourself in the way that seems best to you whether or not it is for your good, both immediately and for the future. But anyway, you've grown older and wiser, and I've been attempting to slide my little light beside yours—though it was often almost extinguished by the activities which you've put forth and the ideas that you've poured out. You should know that those things which are in line with the destiny of your path will work out for you in spite of the fact that you might wish to push them away, and all in all, we're going to help as you stumble your way forward.

One thing more: Please realize that I am not living your life for you! I, George Felbers, am a being, even as are you, finding my way over here, just as you're finding your way there. The ideas I have, the mistakes I make, the things I promulgate are the things which I see as best to do even as do you. If you have decisions to make, ideas to express, or ways to make yourself harmonious with your environment, you are allowed to stumble and bumble, finding your own way.

It isn't easy, living as you do—sensitive, reactive, and often alone in your thinking, apart from the ideas of your fellow men. But I assure you, it is a good way for you and for those of you who are understanding of spirit communication—and the realization of life going on after death.

I can pluck thoughts as they radiate out beyond your mind and brain, utilizing them in a way that I am able to do through training, understanding, and communication experiments in the ages past. I am able to project thoughts to you in a rather unusual manner because of our karmic ties in other lives. The present dispensation for you allows a great deal of spiritual influence in your life. You are to have the help of spirit people always, in everything you do. You will not be alone.

In the pact, you stated, prior to coming onto the earth plane, that you would become a fellow creature of spiritual understanding and comprehension. Thus the spirit people could give their message through you and for any others that would listen. Perhaps those who would listen may not be many, but they are important. You see, each person has a role to play on the stage of life when they enter the physical plane. Your role is to find people who accept the fact, as you do, that there *are* spirit people, as well as a spirit world, anxiously awaiting contact with others through you.

This is George with you now, having a fine time, making good contact, and saying, God bless you, Rib. You are right for us and we for you.

Goodbye for now, George speaking.

With this message, George had reiterated that the universe worked according to a natural, a *spiritual*, law. And Riblet was shocked to learn that George had specifically died at an early age so that he would be in the spirit world to aid Riblet while he lived his life in the physical world. As Rib considered this possibility, he was reminded of the unexpected passing of his mother, and of the young woman he had loved, bringing the emotion from those experiences to the surface. Did this mean, he wondered, that the souls of these loved ones had left the physical plane early in order to perform some particular work on the other side?

And just what was the work that Rib and George were meant to do? "Together," George had said, "we can help to expel the darkness from the lives of some people on earth." Apparently, Rib was to pass along the lessons he was learning to whomever would listen. But when he considered his life and work as a professional man in this small town, it seemed impossible that he had some spiritual destiny on this plane. Truly, as George had acknowledged, it wasn't easy for Rib, living as he did, often alone in his thinking and frequently isolated from the ideas of his fellow man. Fortunately he had more messages to come.

chapter 8

COMMUNICATION BETWEEN THE TWO WORLDS

In the following out-of-body experience an extraordinary two-way communication takes place when a patient, now newly born on the other side, wished for a visit with someone from the earth plane.[1] Riblet was aware that the patient, before his death, believed firmly that there was no life after death, and Rib anticipated a difficult adjustment for this gentleman who found himself living on, although in another environment. It was for this reason that Rib made a prayerful request to help this individual if such aid was called for.

Visit to a Former Patient

I commenced the slow, rhythmic breathing that always precedes my pulling out of the body. The languid, pleasant sense of spiritual peace stirred through my being. A deep sigh, a soft exhalation—I was at peace, but not yet free of the body.

Now I was aware of George standing at my side. Beside him stood Dr. Sommers [a physician in the spirit world who frequently accompanied Riblet on his out-of-body journeys]. I roused out of my body and stretched out an arm to each of them, which they took to steady me. They pulled me gently up and forward, and I felt myself free, but with a strong pull back to the body. I took a step forward and away and felt the pull less strongly.

Now a short intervening period of obliviousness, and I found myself in a lovely park, surrounded by many beautiful evergreen trees, tall and graceful and majestic. I was sitting on a stone bench between George and Dr. Sommers. They were still holding my arms and wrists as they had when I had first left the body.

I still was not poised and free from the physical body sensations. I had not yet the etheric freedom that I must have for my journey or mission, whatever it might be. I intuitively knew this and was aware that the quiet rest here in this park was for the purpose of better spirit orientation. As we sat there, I was aware of spasmodic jerking of my body, back on the earth plane. My hands and fingers seemed to close convulsively. But soon a deeper peace was apparent; deeper rhythmic breathing and better relaxation ensued.

Now I felt free to turn to the duties at hand. Without a word being spoken, I signified my ease, and together we started down a path through the park to a building that could be seen in the distance.

As we approached this structure, it seemed somewhat like a beautiful modern hospital, except that it carried a look and feeling of an elegant home rather than an institution. We climbed several steps to reach the entrance. As I climbed, it seemed that the reactions and vibrations of my etheric body changed, because by the time I had reached the top of the short flight of steps I was more nearly attuned to the spiritual vibrations of the plane upon which I was presently active. I seemed now to know the purpose of our visit and whom we would find and converse with there.

We entered the large, resplendent reception room and office. Beautiful furnishings and a soft light created such a glow of quiet and rest that I can even now feel the peace expressed there. I walked to the desk of the attendant seated there in the room and stated my mission, telling her that I was only an earthly visitor, freed temporarily from the physical body and could remain only a short time. She beckoned me to follow her, and the group of us left this comfortable room and walked through a large doorway to an impressive court. . . .

I now seemed to be perfectly aware of this place and what its purpose was. I even now knew that I was here in answer to an earnest little prayer I had prayed relative to a patient who had recently made his transition, rather suddenly and unexpectedly. I had asked that I might know of this person's spiritual status and that if I could be of any assistance to enlighten him as to his new life, I be permitted to help. I knew of this newborn soul's disbelief of the reality of the spirit world. Now I knew my prayer was being dramatically answered!

As a digression, at my last attendance of this patient, I was intuitively aware of his impending transition even though his physical signs seemed to point to the contrary. I had clairvoyantly seen the gentleman's spirit father and grandfather standing at his side with a look of pleading anxiety in their faces. Now, here I was, on an intermediate spirit plane, in a resting house in the spirit world, visiting a newly transitioned spirit!

The environment was magnificent beyond physical possibilities, and the spirit was being given just that spirit reaction which he had earned in earth life. I seemed to know exactly where I would find him. The four of us paused at the door of his apartment, and upon his welcoming signal, entered. . . .

The gentleman came forward to meet me, surprise written clearly on his face. Obviously it seemed incomprehensible to him that he could be greeting me. I read from his thoughts that he knew he was "dead" and he was not too tolerant of the fact!

Now he spoke rapidly, asking me many questions. I tried to give him all the reassurance I could about the reality of his new life in the etheric planes. We sat and for a short while discussed his transition. He told me how he had felt, what had occurred after the passing, and he even knew about the arrangements for the burial of his body. He knew also of the contents of the funeral oration which had been spoken for him.

At first he had denied, with bewilderment, some of his transition experience, but now knew that the part relating to future spiritual life was true. I drew several conclusions for this spirit friend, which he eventually accepted and acted upon. He knew that the need for continued activity was certain, and he felt that he could somehow learn to make the necessary adjustment to the new life.

So, soon I was ready to leave him; my mission, I thought, was successful. It seemed that for the utter conviction of his soul, he had wanted to talk with someone from earth life—then, he said, he would willingly carry on in this new plane of existence. The request had been granted him. I was the one whereby contact was made, and a newly born spirit was placed thereby into constructive activity.

He followed us out of his apartment, expressing his pleasure at seeing a known earth being. We looked about us at the beauty of the open court with the fountain playing so enchantingly. He breathed a sigh of contentment. I turned to leave and knew that all was now well with the soul of this newly born spirit.

We passed quietly out of this resting home and again down the steps into the park. I spoke a quiet message of thanks for the help of my friends in spirit and for the privilege of being there with them, free of the physical body and earth plane. I knew my mission was completed. The pull to earth grew strong again.

This counseling session between Riblet and his patient is a revealing illustration of how information is conveyed from one plane to the other. Looking over his journal the next evening, Rib read about the encounter and wondered about the various forms of communication between himself, his guide, his relatives, and, of course, his patients on the other side.

As might be anticipated, George had quite a lot to say about communication between the spirit world and the earth plane in general, and between himself and Riblet in particular. In the following recorded message, he speaks of several methods of contact between the two planes. And unlike earlier messages, here George, at times, seems to speak directly to the reader.

Communication

RIBLET: This is Sunday, about ten o'clock in the evening. As I am reading, I am very impressed with the closeness of the psychic realm around me now, and I know the spirit people are much interested in scientific thoughts. I wouldn't mind if George would occasionally jump in with some ideas and expand some of his understanding relating to the psychic world—his world.

GEORGE: I want to explain that when I come to you, it is as though you are in a dual consciousness—you are semi-entranced. You are responsive to my thoughts, and you express them your way. You know what I'm saying, but seem far away from the words spoken. It is as though you were speaking through a distant telephone. You hear the words and voice them, but still you do not seem to be a part of them.

Communication of the spirit world with the physical plane of life is of much more consequence than one would be allowed to believe. Few people will accept—and it is a fact of life—that communication with the other realm is as natural a phenomenon as is the factor of radio and television. . . .

You know, many people who come over here know nothing about communication. Much time must be spent in teaching them the value of communication and even the reality of it! Teachers and those who are experts in life—pertaining to communication with the various realms and planes of existence as we find them here—do the instructing when it's called for.

In addition I want to tell you that you are also being helped by certain technicians. They have learned through the study of communication, on this side, a means of passing a thought, or impressing you better than we might. I am actually the communicator, not the only communicating intelligence. The thoughts that are being brought through to you, and which you are now expressing, come from a group of experts over here who are versed in the lines of communication in a manner that is not ordinarily understood by the people, even in my world. Understand that people there, where you are, have the willingness to communicate, but do not have the means or understanding of how it can be produced or reproduced. And so it is over here. The things that I am telling you now are given you with the aid of these so-called technicians, here, where I am. The work that I have done has been through concentration, experimentation, and through learning of the laws concerning communication—and the laws of life—on my side.

Now, I would like to say something about *psychic rainfall*. That sounds a bit strange, but when I explain my concept of it, I think you'll understand what I mean. You know, in your plane of life, you anticipate rain showers, heavy windblown storms, or light, soft droplets, like fog. All of these things are different aspects of physical resolution of moisture in your physical life. Well, corresponding to that, I might say that over here in the psychic world there is something similar—that is to say, there are showers of psychic rainfall. I think a good sensitive would be aware when he was in a psychic atmosphere where psychic rainfall was falling. There are electromagnetic spots in your physical plane that correspond to similar ones on the plane of life where I am. If the conditions are such that the downpour or the intensification of this psychic force may be made manifest, it will be there; and anyone who walks into it will be affected by it, whether he's conscious of it or not.

To illustrate, you've all been in places where you have felt as though there was something in the air, or that you anticipated something about to move in your way—but you could not speak of it with true knowledge. These could be areas you might wander into, which would open your psychic senses sufficiently to make you aware of the things that might be close to you.

I'd like to have Riblet know that he is much more closely surrounded by psychic forces than he realizes. He is almost constantly in the psychic atmosphere. Psychic ramifications are always penetrating his thoughts and ideas—which he can pick up and utilize if he chooses to do so. We're glad that we've now entered an active stage of his psychic existence, for that's what he came here to do. He's going to do it to a greater degree than he can see at this time.

The psychic world is with you very much more than you realize. The more you are able to comprehend the fact that you are guided and aided by unseen forces, beings, and even magnetic ramifications of power, you'll see that there is a great deal more to your lives than may appear to you.

Another type of communication I want to explain is the *psychic bridge.* I want you to understand there is a modus operandi, a faculty whereby you get into our realm, the psychic realm, with ease—that is, through the psychic, or etheric, bridge. It is a means, really—a way. It is an example of the mind acquiring knowledge that it knows nothing about, which it could obtain through its physical senses. And this is used a great deal more readily than one would be allowed to recognize. It is understood by sensitives, to a greater or lesser degree, and is utilized as freely as possible by those who are conscious of it.

The positive psychic uses the etheric bridge through the conscious mind, pulling in images, as compared to others who do not understand the rules governing the communication— who would be gathering impressions through auras, atmospheric vibrations, or sensations that are apparent everywhere and are a part of both our worlds.

Still another important form of communication is known as *radiation.* In fact, one of our methods of approaching you from our world to yours is in this manner. You've read something of the aura, that envelope of color about each person, and you realize that the radiation of the personality or the extension of one's thoughts and emotions goes far beyond the limitations of the personality of the physical vehicle that you're using at the present time. Well, I want to tell you that, over here, we utilize this same force of radiation to contact you. It's much like striking a match and lighting a candle in the darkness. Before the match is struck, before the candle is lighted, there may be total or relative darkness. But with the lighting of the candle, a certain degree of the darkness is taken away. There will be a glimmer, a phosphorescent glow which may be apparent to both spirit people and to those on the earth plane.

This radiation of energy coming from the sun that gives life to the plants, the animals, and even you, is a subtle, mysterious, unknown quantity and quality of force, or spiritual power; and yet it is very active in your lives. You cannot see the growth as the sun radiates and emanates light, how it is absorbed and utilized by plants, animals, and man. You cannot know the power of the radiation of one spirit person to another. You cannot realize that even we here in the spirit world depend on the radiation process to reach you or to reach others in our plane of life, but this is often the case. Just as you recognize the radiation or the *presence* of a person near you who would express a certain mood, you would sense that mood and receive it. How do you receive it? Through radiation.

And so it is with our approach to you. The things that you learn from the spirit world will come to you through radiation as well as through thought transference, wherein we may be able to give you suggestions. In addition, because you must become more and more aware of our presence and be consciously aware of us, this radiation will be a very great part of your work on the physical plane—before you come over here with us. You must also learn to look to the Source, to the power of God, the majesty of the presence of the spiritual power that is in you, through you, around you, and at your side, constantly mingling through the very cells of your body.

We want to teach you to recognize more and more consciously this great spiritual power, which may be recognized as a light. Those who can attune sufficiently to you to be aware of this radiation will sense something about your presence that they can receive, both consciously and unconsciously. The more developed spiritually a person may be, the better he or she will be able to react to your radiation. And, of course, the more he or she is able to radiate spiritual power himself, the more you will be attracted to and understand his presence. . . .

Each time you meditate, every little prayer word that you send out to us or to anyone in the spirit world or to the Source itself, is an emanation, a radiation that becomes light, which becomes power, a factor to reckon with. Nothing is too small to be of God, because everything comes from the Source. . . .

You people on the earth plane who are humbly anxious to learn of spiritual reality, often demean yourselves and make yourselves little, in the light of spiritual radiation. You feel you don't have enough power to do much of anything, that what you do is of no consequence, and the little bit that you can contribute to world affairs is so minute as to make it negligible. We hasten to assure you from our world—this is not so! Everything has been placed where it is placed and in a certain manner so that all may interact and harmonize, and so that God, in His great wisdom, may carry on this onward-moving power of Himself.

Just be yourself. Aspire to becoming a lighthouse, a guidepost whereby others may feel the light and be blessed. In that way, they will light their own little candles of spiritual power, radiating whatever light they may have for the benefit of other souls on the earth plane.

George had covered a lot of ground in this message—psychic rainfall, psychic bridges, radiation. It was a lot to take in. But what was of most interest, perhaps, to Riblet as a physician, was George's statement: "Those who can attune sufficiently to you to be aware of this radiation will sense something about your presence that they can receive, both consciously and unconsciously. The more developed spiritually a person may be, the better he or she will be able to react to your radiation." This seemed to explain what so many of Riblet's patients reported. Again and again they spoke of a "warmth," a "glow." "I could always feel this intense warmth," his patient Diana Peterson had said, "right on the very spot where it hurt the worst. . . . It's intense and it just sort of develops—a good warm feeling that is sustained for some time afterward." And William Clearly had said he felt as if Riblet's hand was inside his body when he treated his back. "I felt a glow inside afterward," he said.

There was clearly a beyond-the-physical-world communication taking place between Riblet and his patients. It seemed that he naturally radiated warmth and healing through his hands, and also that certain of his patients were, at least subconsciously, attuned to that radiation—and accepting of it. A powerful healing combination—Riblet's radiation and the acceptance by certain patients of that healing power.

In addition, from what George had said, we could conclude that these patients had been attracted to Riblet, had sought him out for treatment, because of some unconscious awareness of his power; and, further, that the patients and Riblet had probably been guided by the spirit world to find one another.

After listening to the tape with his friend Charles, Riblet was excited about all the information he had received. The two men discussed the contents of the message and decided that it really all came back to George's comment: "The psychic world is with you on the physical plane, guiding and aiding more than you realize."

And further direct communication with the psychic world would indeed guide Riblet; in his future lay a journey to the so-called lower realms, and a very unexpected psychic visitor.

chapter 9

FATE, FREE WILL, AND A
VISITOR FROM A HIGHER PLANE

Despite George's messages, as Rib continued to live through his various spiritual adventures, he still questioned the reasons for his being chosen for the kind of life he was living. From time to time, he had his doubts. Nevertheless, wanting to learn something about fate and our existence on the earth plane, one Sunday morning Riblet asked his guide to come through. And George was glad to accommodate.

George Talks about Fate and Free Will

RIBLET: This is Sunday, a winter's morning, about 9:30 A.M. It's a dull, dismal day outside, but this morning I've had splendid contact with the etheric world. I was very much interested in the thoughts that George was conveying to me today regarding something concerning fate and the line of life force that governs each one of us individually. I'd like to have him express himself this morning—something about fate and life and all those things that have to do with our existence here on the earth plane. I'm going to try to sleep, within my own consciousness, and let George record those things he wishes to say so that I may hear them when I wake up.

GEORGE: Good morning. This is George speaking. I am glad to talk. I want to tell you something about this thing you call fate, and how it is that your lives are governed, by lines of force and lines of light that have to do with your experiences on the earth plane. I told you many times, and I'm sure you're aware, that fate is a reality. Your lives are governed according to the laws of spiritual reality in association with the powers of life as they are expressed—through thought, emotion, and through the expressions of thinking and doing on your physical plane.

I'd like to have you know that the lines of life, as they express themselves to each of you individually, are according to your existence in association with the experience that you have had in the spirit world prior to coming to earth existence. The things that are affecting you now, as you're living adult lives in the physical plane, have to do with your reaction to the experiences that are placed before you.

Life experience is a magnificent, ongoing force, of which you can have but slight cognizance and understanding at this time because you are seeing through the eyes dimly and through the mind vaguely—the reason being that you're getting a limited perspective of life as it actually is. You know of course that your five physical senses limit you. They do not exactly expand your consciousness. While they hold you away from the world of reality, it is through the limitations of these senses—as you are born in the physical body—that you gain experience. That is to say, you are led into things that *may happen* to you, and by your reaction to those opportunities and challenges that are placed before you, the reactions of other things to come will follow. There will be experiences that will be in line with the destiny of your life. You may have earned such occurrences, or you may have been placed where these activities can work best for you. According to your reaction to those happenings, through your choices, the things that affect you are set up for experiences to come.

In occult literature, there is an oft-quoted statement which I think is frequently misunderstood. That statement says, "When the student is ready, the teacher appears." Well, if you would consider that the teacher is *experience*, and when the student is in line with the life force of his existence, in a true manner, then he's going to gain from the experiences that befall him. He will be given the opportunity to make choices, and those choices, with the subconscious knowledge and the superconscious understanding that is within his being, he will choose according to the life path on which he is placed.

It's very interesting, isn't it, to comprehend that of all the billions and billions of souls that inhabit the universe, not only this universe but many other universes also, that each soul is unique and individual, a being apart? That is to say, no other experience will be like his. The choices he makes will be unique, and that which may befall him will be like no other. Please remember that you, as a child of God, are forging your own way, shining your own light, and being your own you.

I did have to come over here to learn something of the light of ongoing spiritual progress, and something having to do with the laws of communication between our world and yours. Through those things, I have learned to value the blessed assurance of the life force of each individual as needed, as wanted, as being a part of the infinite whole.

Just remember this, Riblet. Those things that are *for* you and *with* you are yours to behold because they are uniquely yours, and belong to nobody else. Those things that happen *to* you are according to the background of your destiny of previous experiences—your thinking along certain lines, and your reaction to the laws of life as they affect you only. Through these things, you are gathering together forces which make a light, and that light breaks over, out of your world into the spirit world, and it is the path upon which you will find yourself after you've come over here, after the change called death.

Remember, those things that are for you are yours *now*; you can't get away from them. That is destiny. Call it fate, if you will. But remember that out of all of those things, your choices still remain supreme. God bends His will to your ongoing progress, allowing you the freedom of saying "I do" or "I do not," "I will" or "I will not," "I can" or "I cannot." That is your choice. It is according to your life, according to your light, according to your being. It is for you, where you can glimpse the beauty of the life beyond and see the sunrise of the new day—the reality of life after death.

My blessings again. That is sufficient for now. Think this over and learn to recognize the reality of the grandeur of your soul, and the light of your being, as it exists in relation to the infinite whole—apart from physical disappointments, disillusions, misunderstandings, and negative ideas. There is the Light. There is a spark of the Divine. There is a Reality. There is the Being. You are of God, and all of you are gods in the making.

This is George speaking again, signing off, giving you blessings. Goodbye.

Each life is important and unique, George reminds us, and the choices we make, large or small, do make a difference, on both the physical and spiritual planes.

In the following out-of-body journey, Riblet's visit with a prisoner in the "lower realms" provides a vivid illustration of how the choices we make on the physical plane will follow us to the spirit world. As Rib put it, this experience was "a study in contrasts" as his encounter with the prisoner is followed by a visit to the "higher realms," where he is given a glimpse of what life was like—and can possibly be again—on earth.

A Lower Realm, the Children, and the Teacher

It was 3:30 P.M. and I was alone in my bedroom. The subject was a study in contrasts of planes in the spirit world. Ordinarily, when I projected I went out through the head, but this time the whole body went forward; so I knew I was getting into a different experience than I'd been in before. After the pull-out was completed, we seemed to travel in a straight line, not leaving the earth plane. Vibrations were heavy and thick, and a tendency to nausea was in my body. A heavy weight was on my solar plexus. Finally we found ourselves at a prison. I heard sounds of cursing and moaning and groaning before we reached the place.

All was very dense, with heavy fog—like milk, it was so thick. The moans and curses grow louder, and finally I see dimly, the figure, alone in an ordinary prison cell. Facing the cell bars is a man sitting on a cot with his head in his hand. He is in a highly emotional state, muttering and groaning. About him I see the thought pictures that he has produced in the ether.

I think his name was Miller [while on the earth plane].[1] He does not know that he has gone through death and is in the spirit world. His fear of death and intense hatred have stunted his mind until he continually rehearses highly emotional ideas, feelings, and scenes. George tells me he has been electrocuted for killing a man during a bank robbery. He keeps looking back for them to take him to the electric chair.

None of the higher spirit teachers have been able to help him, because they are powerless to do so until he himself is willing to listen; for he alone has the power to regress or advance. It is as he chooses.

The vibrations of the plane we are on and the emotional reaction to the scene have numbed and affected me with faintness, so George calls me and I feel a gradual uplifting out of this oppressing scene. We seemed to soar upwards to a plane of life that was vastly different. We find ourselves in a glorious park, a level expanse of trees and flowers, grass and paths, benches and fountains. The trees which we were under were luminescent as was everything else, as though each thing present furnished its own light rather than depending on an outside sun for illumination.

Presently some very happy children approached, romping and playing as they came. They stopped at a nearby bench, then sat on the grass and wove flowers they had gathered into a long, continuous chain.

Soon one of the children looked up and gave a shout of joy. The others glanced to where he pointed and, advancing toward them was a figure clad in a white garment. The face and body of this person was radiant and emitted a brilliant white light. As he came toward the children, they ran to him and begged him for a story. He took several of them on his lap, and the rest gathered on the grass at his feet. Then in a voice that was low and glorious and vibrant, he told them, in exquisite allegory, the following "tale."

"Long ago, when the earth was young, all the children of God walked the earth even as do you here. There was peace and happiness everywhere. But gradually, conditions began to change. Men started to cut themselves apart from their divine natures and, for selfish reasons, began to accumulate wealth so as to make themselves superior to their fellow beings. This was the beginning of shadows to form upon the earth. Before that time, all was luminous, as you see it here. But gradually the Spirit Light began to die out, and men began to depend on the material sun for illumination."

At this point, his narrative ceased as to words and gradually we heard, coming from the atmosphere all around us, chanting of many children's voices. The attending children looked up into the atmosphere with intent, eager faces.

Soon we saw forming in clouds above the head of the speaker beautiful, exquisite pictures illustrating what he had to say. George and I stood, intent and interested in the presentation. There we saw outlined to us the picture of the world's so-called progress from the time of the perfection of the earth, through the periods of the lessons learned by different races of men on down to the present day.

We saw the chaos and destruction. We saw the clouds and dark shadows, all caused by man's perversity. And gradually there faded into our view the picture of present-day chaos. Out of this there evolved a great white light. This we seemed to know was representative of Truth, and as such, only this light could lead us out of our present difficulties. But how could this be? Only through proper knowledge of higher spiritual forces— by recognizing ourselves as children of God, slowly, laboriously climbing out of the darker planes of self and degradation.

The darker planes were represented by the criminal seen in spirit in his cell, while the higher realms of peace and happiness and joy were represented by the teacher and the little ones.

The stark contrast between the two visits left Riblet shaken. This was his only experience in the lower realms, and as he thought about the deplorable state of mind of the prisoner—who, of course, had an option but didn't realize it—he learned once more about the importance of the choices we make.

This particular lesson was expanded upon with the channeled appearance of Jules Juret (pronounced Zhu-RAY), a spirit master of high standing, and a Frenchman with a marked accent. Jules appeared only this one time, and through his existence Riblet learned that he could give voice to someone other than George.

In George's preliminary remarks it is obvious that he is speaking, as he has done before, to an audience other than Rib—perhaps directly to the you, the reader.

Words from a Higher Being—Jules Juret

GEORGE: Good evening, Riblet. This is George. We're going to do something different tonight that Rib doesn't know about. He doesn't know what's coming—which is probably an unfortunate thing, catching him off guard. This will give me a chance to operate with him, doing more of control, in a formal way. I'm going to wait a bit, so I may take over better control of his vehicle. We will hold silent until I have opportunity to come back again. . . .

Now I've got control. I'm glad I'm here; this is like old times I'm glad I'm able to say some of the things that I've wanted to say for such a long time. I know it's late at night, and the kid[2] is not sleepy, so I'm not depriving him of sleep; but we are utilizing the time and quiet of the night to bring out some spiritual ideas and thoughts I've wanted him to study and learn about. Also, I want to introduce a character—a higher being—who does not often *en-trance*. With the help that I may be able to give, he will do so, bringing forth his ideas. We will be quiet for just a moment.

JULES JURET: Hmmmm. Good evening. It is good to see you. This is Jules Juret. I am a teacher of this child, and I am happy to speak again to the earth plane in such a manner that he may hear me. I have lessons that I would offer, so that his work may be understood and utilized better than it is at the present time.

We, over here, look at life differently than you do. We see ourselves as entities of light, perpetuation of God's creation of minuscule vitality. And we understand the limitlessness and the eternity of all, and we know that, in time, we will reach that place. We bring ourselves to fathom what appears to be unfathomable, and we know we will bring ourselves closer to the source of our being.

Existence, as it is in reality—that is, the life force, emanating, pulsating, creating in all its varied forms—is a perpetuation decreed by the Divine Father for the betterment of His children. Ages have passed when time seemed to bear different fruit than it does now, and we watched from afar as there was descending upon this planet the great ones from another world who claimed to instruct the beings of earth, who then were young souls. Out of this descent into matter, from those great cosmic beings of light, fictions, interpretations, and versions of life have grown as it may have started. It was accepted by those on earth who recognized that the creatures about them were different from they and thus, at that time, were considered very holy.

I'm happy to say that I have visited and progressed and worked with those beings from one other planet, and I am about to release more energy into the boy's body so that we may be able to reach out further and receive brighter instructions from the Holy Ones.

You know of course that chance is not a reality. No such thing as happenstance exists. All is in the plan. However, there are variations and individual interpretations and ways of relating power and thought in a certain manner. This gives freedom to the children of earth, so that they may grow and develop under the guidance of those children of light who are supervising the manifestation of life upon this earth plane.

I am privileged to tell you that there is much cataclysmic destruction coming upon this earth in a way which you may not understand. This will be a result of the combined forces of nature, as the thought forces have gone out, coalesced, and driven themselves into a reality that has given them an independence. These forces of nature follow the thoughts of man in a degree much closer than you perhaps realize. You have reached a place in the progress of the planet where there will be the dividing path, and many choices will be made, *must* be made, by men and women now incarnated on the earth plane, as to which path to take. I assure you that the power of Spirit is a ruling force of the universe. By that, I mean there are frequencies of force, dynamic power, a radiation of energy, expansion of consciousness, and awareness in intuitive powers, that are at work on the earth plane, even though few people realize that those things may be so. Yet they are real. They guide your nation, and they bring forth that which must be, according to the seeds which have been sown.

The Holy Book, one of the Holy Books, which I have studied through many eons, contains those words which we all know, "As ye sow, so shall ye reap." And so it *must* be. And you, my friends on the earth plane, are now living in a time of reaping. There will be further extensions of that power which will rebalance the opposing forces of negative thinking, doing, and being, so that there will be a challenge in such a manner that one man may judge himself entirely in conflict with such opinions. Still, through all of this must come this balancing.

It has been decreed that the laws of mankind—which work with and without man's aid—will govern his existence on the earth plane only so long as there is sufficient balance so that souls may migrate to your world, your earth plane, and learn therefrom. When the imbalance is of too great a degree, the law requires destruction and a new beginning, such as comes about through the millennial changes that you have read about and talked about in times past.

It is fine to be with you, and I am joyous in the realization that there are some of you who are looking to the light. There are many of you who are realizing the power of Spirit alive within your breasts. With meditation and heartfelt prayer you can allow the power of Spirit within you to manifest—to dominate your life in a way that you will know that you are of spiritual origin—so that you will go on into other worlds when you meet your so-called death on the physical plane.

How interesting that word death. You on the earth plane shy away from that word, possibly because of misunderstanding. But it is an essential part of life, for change takes place only when one form becomes uninhabitable, and the mother envelope of power must take its place. When the crossing over is complete—with the person who has the light in his heart so that he knows of the power of Spirit—he is given guidance by those enlightened ones who await his coming. He is assigned particular areas where he can best develop his own abilities, desires, and expectations. He is placed in the great universal scheme of life. He, as a key member of reality of Spirit, will be able to help others who are less advanced upon the path on which we all tread.

We also want you to know that the life that is lived on the earth plane is for a specific purpose: *Rather than agreeing to a selfish demonstration of power, it is for learning to master your emotions and thoughts and learn a willingness to give of self for the benefit of others.*

Many men and women of your age do not see the light in this manner and thus they may be consumed in the great conflagration, with the changing of planetary conditions. There will be a mingling of the power of those who know, with the younger souls who are blindly stumbling along the path.

It is not often that I may speak thus to you, my son. I choose at this time to tell you that we are watching carefully the things you do, hoping you will be kind to your body. Give of your best maintenance of power to those who need it, without the sacrifice of self. We want you to know that the balance of life is in your hands. You hold the key, and you possess the power to make decisions that will determine those things which may activate the environment before you and bring you to the place where you need to be for lessons to be learned.

It is wonderful to recognize, my lad, that you are on the path, stepping slowly, haltingly, upward, unto the light; and that you are seeing the vastness of the universe from a new comprehension and a new wisdom. The years which sit lightly upon your head are the years of determination of future activity, for you have placed before you your vessel of service, and it is filled and blessed by the higher beings above.

I go now; others will be here. It is good to greet you. This is Jules Juret, and I say adieu.

GEORGE: Well, I'm back again, Riblet, and I'm glad we were able to make contact again, much in the old manner. It's good to know that the progress has gone on in the work that we were to do—whether or not you have listened to the things that I have suggested or to the pleadings that I have made to you at various times.

We are now awaiting a period wherein there will be a transition which will affect you in a manner that will arouse your illumination to the pitch of really understanding the force of life as it sweeps aside the activity called death. This will bring into play magnificent manifestation of true Spirit Power. The gulf between your world and ours has grown shallower and shorter, and the distance is not so far; but before you come to where we live, you must continue with your mission and do that which is for you to do.

Allow me to offer a prayer before I leave: "Father, we thank Thee that Thou hast seen fit to apply the Light of Love in such a manner that radiation may be a dominant factor which will enable mankind to climb up higher in spiritual power, to see vistas of Light and Love in such a way that peace may finally be established upon the earth plane and in the lower reaches of the spirit world, so that the power of God may dominate. Amen."

It's good to have been here. It was a privilege. And now I think I should release you, Riblet, and I bid you adieu. We will meet again soon. Goodbye, George.

It seemed that with each entrancement, more spectacular information and characters came to Riblet. With the new information he had just received from George and Jules, as well as from his own visit with the prisoner and the teacher in his out-of-body experience, Riblet began to understand the magnitude of Jules's comment, "The balance of your life is in your hands." As children of God—"gods in the making," as George had put it—our choices literally *create* the world around us. Jules's statement, then, that life "is for learning to master your emotions and thoughts and learn a willingness to give of self for the benefit of others" took on new meaning.

And yet, again, Riblet was anxious to talk to someone about the questions and doubts raised by these most recent encounters. And as before, he didn't dare to share such information with his small circle of friends, at least not until there was a time that he could play the recording and let them judge for themselves. And so feeling a bit lonely and isolated, he could only keep his thoughts to himself.

chapter 10

SOUL SEARCHING
AND SOUL GROWTH

For two days, Riblet had been ill with the flu and was only seeing patients occasionally. He was in a pensive mood, still soul searching and in turmoil over his continuing conflict regarding the reality of George. Now, at one of his lowest points, he received inspiration and support from a combination of sources: George, the writings of a world-famous psychic and medium, and a lucid dream—a type of dream in which the dreamer remains "awake" and cognizant that they are in a dream.

Riblet clearly sensed the significance of the low point he was in, and felt a need to record the happenings of those hours. The following is the lucid dream he recorded that day.

The Lucid Dream and Jane Roberts

[Sleepily] Well, it's 12:30 A.M., and this will be a weird tape. I doubt if I'll ever get another just exactly like this, because

I want to record my impressions and things that happened with me, and to me, through the day. It's been an unusual period. I've been sick, in bed all day yesterday, with medicine, and had Charles call my patients and excuse me, which I hate like hell to do. But I did it, knowing it was the best thing to do and I spent my day quietly. When I was awake, I was reading a new book, *The Seth Material* [by Jane Roberts].[1]

I like this book; it comes nearer reading me—with my doubts, hesitations, and bewilderment—yet bringing joy, and happiness. I know inside of me, to the very depth of me, the soul of me which goes beyond the ego, the soul of me which knows its truth, and I know now—I had to be middle-aged to know it—that communication with George is possible. It isn't a figment of my imagination nor is he an alter ego, or a subconscious entity which I've built up to make things seem real to me. I *know* George is *he*, a real person.

Well, I want to tell about this dream. It's affected me all day. It's enlightened me. It's lifted me. It's given me the go-on signal. And it makes life seem simpler. I'm buoyant. I'm in love with life. If I could go through the rest of my life with this feeling, this particular feeling of having *got it*, of *knowing*, I couldn't ask for more!

Anyway . . . I lay down on the davenport and opened the book, to the chapter on dreams, and this chapter mentioned that you worked out your philosophy first through dreams, making them actual and real. If that didn't work, then it was transferred over onto your body through sickness, meaning that something wasn't right, that the evidence pointed to the fact that you'd slipped a cog somewhere, that your engine, your motor, your body, wasn't running right, and the sickness was a result of that. I must say, I accepted that, and I know it's true, and I loved reading this, thinking about the facts as they were presented to me.

Well, this is the dream that I want to expound about because it's lifted my day. Gosh, I believe it's made a difference with my philosophy of life! If I can hang onto it, I'll do good with the rest of my work, especially my spiritual healing. Anyway, I seemed to be awake, and yet I knew I wasn't. I was in a square room, a big square room, and it was white and it was light, and I said, "Why, there isn't any darkness; it's all light!" I was awake enough that I looked at the clock and it was a little before 5 A.M. It was still dark outside and really looked black. It was raining too, although that didn't enter the picture.

I was in this great, huge white room. My spirit got a lift out of it. I felt I was right with the world; it was good. And there before me were three massive shell-like objects. I can scarcely describe them. They seemed to be like shells that were round and had configurations on them, like balloons with stripes. That's what they seemed to be—three of them sitting in a row in front of me, right where you exited from the room.

These seemed to be important, although what they were I do not know. But I got a good *lift* out of them. I seemed to think, "Gosh, the world's light, and I'm in it and there isn't any darkness. The light's like it ought to be, and things are going to be good because it's white." Everything was white. It was a whiteness that I can't describe. It was different from the blackness of the night which I knew existed right at that time. I was glad to receive it, and I carried this idea and thought with me all day. This whiteness that I was in was real to me, and Jane Roberts, in *The Seth Material*, says that the dream world is a state of consciousness that is just as real as our conscious mind figures out our environment. In other words, the environment of the dream world is just as real, just as *actual*, and it is a part of our being as much as our awakening consciousness is.

I didn't expect to see any patients except one, but after that dream I had energy, I had *life* in me. Doggone, I was kind of bored; I wasn't busy. I had energy to burn, to use, so I saw this one patient at noon because her daughter is being married tomorrow. This wedding is much against her better judgment, but she's powerless to stop it. She leans on me for consolation, and I try to give it to her. We had a very nice talk while I was treating her and I'm sure I helped her as I had wanted to do.

Then I had one other patient who came just for a B-12 shot. That didn't take any energy and I was glad to do it.

Well, I got to thinking about this thing, the dream, all day. It impressed me; it was meaningful. I believe that's true, because I felt it. I felt the consciousness of the light of that room, and this light I lived in, I *absorbed*. And, if I can live *that*, doggone it, it's going to be easy, and to hell with the darkness that's around me and everything else, because the light is real. . . .

Clearly Riblet was buoyed by his experiences that unusual day, and just a few days later, he received the following special Christmas message by George. As he explains, good will that prevails on Christmas day carries over into the spirit world and makes it possible for George's friends on the other side to "do more and accomplish more" than on other days.

Soul Growth

RIBLET: It's 8:30 on Christmas morning. I got up, feeling very close to the spirit world and knowing that this is a day in which communication might be better because of the general manifestation of harmony and good will that is broadcast as a vibration through the earth plane in the realm of thought.

GEORGE: Merry Christmas, Riblet. I'm happy indeed to come this morning to give you greetings from all of us over here to all of you over there.

You are surrounded by a host of those whom you call blesseds on this day, and we are particularly able to get across to you our feelings of love, happiness, harmony, peace, and closeness. Spirit people can come closer to the earth plane on Christmas and do more and accomplish more because we are not held back as much. You celebrate the thought of the birth of the Christ, which is representative of the Spirit of Truth upon the earth, realizing that there is more than appears to be to the physical eye. I would like to have you live the rest of your life with the conscious recognition that the spirit world closely surrounds you at all times, that you are never alone, and that you are comforted and helped and aided in many ways.

The physical plane of life represents one class, one school, one developmental age, wherein the soul grows and prospers and becomes more adept at the great game of living. We recognize that your life as it is lived *now* in physical substance, is for the purpose of gaining knowledge and lessons. You must serve God according to your own soul convictions, with which we cannot and dare not interfere, but we are privileged because it is your destiny and mine that we can come close to you and influence you in ways for the better. Such changes shorten the duration of the experience that you will need prior to advancement into the higher realms of universal life here where I live.

We ask you to stop long enough each day in meditation and thought to call to us and accept our presence and visualize the light of spiritual power as it pours itself about you. You should realize that those spirit people who are helping you really have a great deal more power to aid you than you would suspect, and the more you recognize our presence and allow us to come closer to you, the easier things will be in all aspects of your being.

I'm glad to see you are progressing in the things that you want to do spiritually. There is a law of God which says that like attracts like, and the power of light overcomes the power of darkness. What you are doing now is being done in such a manner that the light is visible to many who are in darkness on my plane. Thus, you are constantly being trailed about by beings who are wanting to see more of the light, to know more of the reality of your being, and to have you help them understand something about the reality of their living after they have passed through what you call death.

Now, I would like to answer some of the questions that have been in your mind, or rather, speak more fully about some things that you have been thinking about. Remember the other day when you had the sudden, overwhelming feeling that all was right with the world? You knew that this was where you should be just at this time, with the overwhelming feeling that you were all right—in where you were, the position you were placed in, and the activities you were undergoing. When you have that sensation of feeling the rightness of things in relation with yourself and the world about you—your world and the physical manifestation of life—it is one of those times in which conditions are appropriate for you to know of your spiritual heritage.

There are points of contact or places of orientation that you must necessarily come to in your lifetime. These may be frequent for some people, and infrequent for many, but certain points of reality must be reached. It is in this point of reality that you will find your true direction in life, and you can go on from there. Yes, we're going to work with you, more and more, through mental and physical phenomena. We will see that you are placed where certain aspects of spiritual power may be presented to you, and you will be led in the desired pathway for the expansion of your awareness of us and the consciousness of true being.

Riblet, we are pleased this morning to make contact again, and as you are aware, our contacts with you are getting better. Yes, we are aiding you in the things you're wanting to do. We are trying to make life as you are living it now a little better for you, a little easier. We hope that at particular times you will be more aware of our presence through phenomena that will help you. You can expand your life into a greater mission of truth for the aid of yourself and your fellow men and those immediately around you.

We're glad to talk again and bring you our peace and happiness and joy for this season. Goodbye. This [with a chuckle] is George, signing off.

Rib absorbed the warm, loving, supportive sensation that he felt in hearing this message from George. It was certainly in keeping with the holiday and the season. He got out of bed with a song in his heart and readied himself for the drive, with his father, to our house. As long as my mother and we children lived in the family home, the whole family, including Sol and Rib, always spent Christmas together. It was one way that Riblet stayed connected with the people he loved in the physical world.

chapter 11

GOD AND
GODS IN THE MAKING

Although Riblet had been raised as a Christian and had even considered a career in the ministry, he once told a friend that he had become a devout materialist for a number of years after leaving his home and parents. Perhaps it was the early letter in automatic writing from his mother, and her mention of God and His works, that had begun to soften Riblet's view on the matter. At any rate, as time went on and he was exposed to and experienced many spiritual and psychic events, Rib began to accept that there had to be a Greater Power. But, he wondered, "If there really is a God, is He a being? How does He work?"

After pondering these questions for some time and thinking about the various messages he had received from George, Rib decided one evening to ask for help in gaining a better understanding of God.

George Speaks about God

RIBLET: I've been meditating and thinking about how the universe works and how God oversees all that goes on, if indeed that is the case. I've felt George's presence, so perhaps he'll answer some of these questions I've had.

GEORGE: Good evening, Riblet. I heard your question, and I believe I can help you in your thinking about God and your relationship to Him. As you know, I was a young man just twenty-three years old when I came over here, and I had much to learn about God, the same as most other newly born spirits.

It is when active faith dares to believe God to the point of action that something has to happen. Believe in this, Riblet. Know that God works to the farthest point of the universe, to the farthest point in your life, to the farthest way that can be conceived by man—God works for you.

All your life you've been attempting, in some way, to live according to a pattern of life as you think it should be lived, according to the way you want to express it. Now is the time to consciously comprehend the power of life in a way that would guide and help you live reality, and teach you power and wisdom and truth beyond your comprehension. This can aid you in setting aright a miraculous power—everything that is good for you and everyone around you.

You should recognize by this time that God is a force, a power to be reckoned with—something of which no power may counteract. It's reality—He is you. He is in everything. He is through everything. He is the now. He is the past. He is the

136

future. He is a radiation. He is something quite apart from a being, and yet He has personality. He has love, and He has genuine concern for each minute cell of activity of life in the spirit world and on the physical plane, too. God in His ramification of power sees fit to gently hold that touch of a bird, that wee one when it leaves the nest. He has the power of the tremendous force of nature at work in wind and water. He works according to that plan which He created some time in the past, so far back that no one knows the origin of it.

Consider God as a thrusting, loving light, a power of wisdom. This power is Divine Energy, a force so huge and magnificent that your little finite mind cannot comprehend what it is and what it isn't. Suffice it to say that God *is*. God is wisdom first. You should have wisdom because you are a part of God. You should have an understanding of life, which is magnificent beyond anything you can comprehend; which is greater than the rising and setting of the sun; which is greater than all the forces of the universe—that's God. You're a god in the making. You're great, powerful, and magnificent.

To use unfairly any little part of the universe is being unfair to God. Bless those who misunderstand you, who enjoy doing other than what you may think right, who live life according to *their* ideas. They are also parts of God, perhaps living unknowingly, in a negative manner, but living as gods in the making, even as you are.

I'd like to get across to you tonight the power, the magnificence of the reality of God's very presence living within you, making the possibility that you need only stretch forth your hand to have seeming miracles occur. Such is often the case when the power of God can come through you uninhibited. You are able to do great things, whether you know it or not. You *have* done great things, *but you can do more*.

Help yourself to know that unseen beings are often at your side, gently suggesting to you things which may be for your good or aiding you in trusting toward better manipulation of your energy. Help yourself to be humble before the power of God. Each time you touch a patient, know that you, as an individual, are but a vehicle through which His infinite power and healing force can flow.

Healing force is a great objective in your life. We want to help you bring it into full, fruitful reality, whereby, with a touch, you may be able to heal others; whereby with a thought, you may be able to make others feel infinitely better physically, mentally, spiritually, and every way. Know that the Great Being, God, has blessed you with a certain power, enabling you to carry forward the vibrations of health and help and wholeness in ways not given to everyone, but ways which are there to be had, for the asking. Pray often; seek the silence.

All healings will not come to you. All fruitfulness may not be yours. All perfection is something toward which you must thrust yourself. The peace of God, the love of all of us over here in spirit, and the wholeness of your life will fulfill your mission on earth, and we will have it so, until you come over here with us.

You know of your background, of the God in you. You know of pinpointing the power of the past into a physical body such as you have now. You know you can use this aid for the good of yourself and for others. I ask that you follow the way before you, as you have, down through the ages past, toward the fulfillment of the expression of the whole—the Godhood working through you, with you, and for you.

Your life may be such that some things will not be as you would wish. At times you may feel yourself frustrated and held down—and even abandoned by me, George. Such will not be the case. Always, we will be with you, inspiring you, helping you look forward to the new day, aiding you and transposing your thoughts into spiritual accomplishment, knowing that the love, the peace, and the power of God is your birthright. Accept that birthright, Riblet.

There can be no negative force. Negative force is only undeveloped good. Power of life is yours. Power of darkness is unenfolded light. Simplify your life to the point where you may know that God is within, without, through you, and manifesting Itself in ways beyond your comprehension. Give yourself over to being and doing that which is good. Always prepare yourself to receive impulses of divine origin, intuitive ways whereby you may encounter wisdom.

Enable yourself to enlarge your vision of life. Spread joy and contentment and peace within yourself, so it will be mirrored, a picture to those about you. Help yourself live in a positive vein of reality, knowing God is good, and God is love. God is everything. Without Him, there is nothing.

When you come close to God, let God enter you. God is love—love so magnificent that each tiny, little created thing in the universe is a part of Him. He lets each thing work itself out through natural law, not through supernatural law, but through natural law that will include the law of cause and effect. It embraces the laws of love, of understanding, and of peace.

The truth of onward progress, of spiritual awareness—both on the physical plane and over here where I am—all of these things added together spell reality. And in another way, they spell God, because God *is*. There isn't anything else. There aren't any opposing forces to God. He is everything.

Let us say a little prayer: Father, we thank Thee for these things which *are*. We ask that we will all together, knowingly, understand Thy way, and that we can conscientiously say with You, Give us this day our daily bread and forgive us our trespasses. Our minds will not lead us into temptation as we go, but will give us greater power and understanding, blessings, and help forever and ever. Amen.

George speaking. Thank you, Riblet. Good night.

This message indeed gave Riblet a closer look at God—His purpose, His plan—and also at Riblet's own reason for being. And the more he thought about it, the more he was prompted to enrich his spiritual life by reading about others' psychic and spiritual experiences. Rib realized he was not the only person connecting with the spirit world in this way, and he was greatly comforted by this knowledge.

A few weeks after receiving George's message about God, Rib had an even more profound out-of-body experience, as though the heavens had been waiting for his enhanced understanding of the power of God in his life before leading him to the next experience.

The Spiritual Peace Conference

Alone in study. The day is dull, very quiet, snowing. Today I had again a most unusual experience, or more correctly, dual experiences. For I "got out" again today, briefly, away from my body and had a grand time doing it. First, as I lay there reclining in the chair, I felt the delicious numbing, freeing sensation, as of a luxurious stretching of my entire physical body.

Then I was conscious of being just above and away about a foot from the physical body—out in my etheric vehicle. I stepped away a bit, when free, with some difficulty. This time things were entirely different with me. Usually I am not aware of how my body (the astral double) looks as to how it is clothed. But today I noticed it was almost entirely nude, and I was seemingly pulled away from the reclining physical vehicle straight up, away from the restraint only with the help of several other spiritual beings.

At last I was free and as soon as I felt my nudity, George was at hand to provide me with a soft, filmy, gown-like robe, entirely plain and serving as a covering for the entire body. So thus I found myself in my study, standing in my astral body, looking at my physical one, and in company in the room with five other spirit entities. These were men dressed somewhat as

I was, except that the radiance of their robes shone much more brightly than mine.

Three of them I knew: Jules, Dr. Sommers, George, and another I felt the influence from, but he was not in the spirit body there, as I was. The two others were strangers, one evidently a Hindu, as I could see his cream-colored turban very clearly. We all stood there in the room in the presence of my unconscious, entranced physical body. I knew we were waiting to magnetize the spiritual atmosphere better, and that the physical body must be better cared for before we could leave.

Gradually the breathing of my physical body, as I stood looking at it, became more rhythmic and deep, and at a signal from the unknown Hindu personage, we took our departure from the room, all together. We simply commenced to float upward, away and out of the house through the ceiling. Then we found ourselves in the midst of a very animated group of spirit people, and George informed me that we were about to attend a spiritual peace conference wherein would be gathered together representative spirit people from all of the countries of the earth. They were interested in and were investigating a peace movement in the astral regions to counteract the growing hatred of groups of people on earth.

The room was a huge oval enclosure, luxuriously furnished and fitted in exquisite taste. . . . At one end of this beautiful lounge, for so it seemed to be with its soft lights and luxurious chairs placed in well-balanced groups, there extended out into the room a circular platform, it also being exquisitely furnished and softly lighted with no visible source of illumination.

The people here, mingling and conversing pleasantly with each other, fascinated me as being a very representative group. Dispersed amongst both men and women were people of all races and nationalities, each festive and with appropriate dress. Dark-skinned, regal-looking Africans conversed with light-haired, beautiful Nordic-looking beings.

Eastern turbans and brocades contrasted exquisitely with austere dress and decorations of European diplomats. Men whose shining countenances and noble features (who were internationally known figures on earth, before their transition) were in attendance. Surely, few other mortals before me have seen such a host of amazing personalities.

However, it was apparent that the purpose of the conclave was not an ordinary social gathering. A turbaned attendant at the door called a word of silence, and the assembled group became quiet in intense concentration, as with bowed heads they seemed to await the coming of some unseen personage. The light on the stage grew dim and faded out momentarily. Then throughout the room were heard strains of beautiful musical harmony, a masterful composition played by some invisible orchestra which seemed to give to the assembled group a mood of deep reverence and sympathy.

Then the lights glowed brightly and there appeared on the platform, in company with several gentlemen, evidently belonging to the same period, the person of [Benjamin] Disraeli.[1]

As I sit here transposing these notes in the journal immediately following this experience, I do not recall the words of that discourse. I am not aware of the glory of oratory that I heard. I can only carry back with me the knowledge of the earnestness and intense interest of those on the other side. They were endeavoring to tell us blind, deluded souls, still submerged in physical bodies, that we—as an ignorant group of God's children—are *not* cut out of entire contact and communication with the rest of God's vast universe; but we are all parts of one glorious whole, and what affects one group must react and mirror onto others, so that one part of humanity whether incarnate or discarnate cannot progress without the aid of all the rest. *This was the lesson* learned on this trip.

After this experience, after we had left this room in the etheric plane, I began the descent back toward my physical body. Contrariwise to almost all other experiences, this was slow and leisurely, well timed and under control. George descended with me, but I had left the others behind.

Suddenly, in my progress downward, my return was arrested, and I found myself seemingly whirling round and round in midair, as though I was trying to orient myself to some object or location or room. Gradually, out of all of this whirling sensation, I found myself focusing my attention on a beautifully carved mantel that I knew must belong to a specially designed fireplace in some rarely beautiful room.

The whirling gradually lessened and I did find myself, as I seemed mysteriously to know, in a small room or salon of Louis XIV architectural design in which was most artistically blended furniture and furnishings of that period. The room was breathtakingly beautiful in itself. It alone seemed glorious beyond all my ideas of heaven, but to make the heaven complete and to make this experience one to ever live in my consciousness, there in the room sat my arisen etheric mother and her sister, my aunt [Ada], and their stepmother, my grandmother Riblet.

I wish I had words to describe these etheric beings in their superior beauty and perfection. I wish I could somehow make you see these discarnate beings as they really are in all of their natural glory. But my poor words will not do justice to the picture. Suffice it to say that I was there for a few fleeting minutes with them, scarcely even having the time to breathe the words of love that filled our hearts, but at that time I knew them as they really are in their own true home. The mounting emotion of love for them stirred me to the depths of my soul and I could scarcely contain the ecstasy and joy that was mine. I wanted to remain there in that room with them forever, just drinking in the beauty and love that was theirs. Their features, their gowns, the beauty and grace of them, I am unable to describe.

The reaction of this unexpected meeting came rapidly and inevitably, for I found myself no longer able to hold my equilibrium in the etheric body, and so was compelled by the laws governing this experience to make my way earthward again. This time my return and re-contact with the physical body was sudden and intense—painfully so.

I awakened completely jarred and seemed to be gasping for breath. I opened my physical eyes and looked about me, and there smiling a good-natured farewell, with a cheery wave of his hand, was George, my etheric friend, vanishing from my sight.

A last word and he was gone: "Write immediately what you have seen!"

Within a very few minutes, Riblet recovered and began chronicling his encounter. When the writing was completed, he reclined in his easy chair, going over in his mind the many sights he had seen, the extraordinary music he had heard, and the loving and emotional connection with the other world he had felt. He felt, indeed, to be a lucky mortal to be so privileged.

chapter 12

THE TWO WORLDS
AND THE TRANSITION

The three messages from George presented in this chapter are, I believe, the most powerful of all the messages Riblet received from his spirit guide over the years. They overlap and mesh and present a multilayered view of life, death, and the transition between the physical and spiritual worlds.

In the first two discussions, George compares the physical and spiritual worlds and provides a vivid definition of reality.

Comparing the Two Worlds

RIBLET: The hour is early in the morning, and I am meditating and thinking about the spiritual path and the road I know.

GEORGE: Good morning, Riblet . . .

Have you ever stopped to think it through, that you, living on the physical plane of life, are really living in an *intrusion* of the spiritual universe? Pause to comprehend which is the source of your existence. Is it the physical plane? Is this world in which you were born—the physical reality—the dominating factor of your existence?

Stop and reason. Spirit people are universal people. I'd like to have you think along the line of the universe being a spiritual sphere of life force. It isn't physical. It really isn't mental. It's spiritual. By spirit, I mean that you are dealing with the Source of all life. Your Father, God, is a spiritual being, recognizing spiritual attributes which are limitless, enduring forever—omnipotent, omniscient, existing everywhere throughout any force of the universal reality of being.

That's a large order, to think about life existing forever and forever, limitless, and ongoing through eternity. But that's our conception of life over here. We spirit people glimpse a little further into the future than do you. We see life spiraling onward and in a way that you may not recognize now. Nonetheless, the ongoing force of spiritual power is the one, true, universal power of reality.

The world in which I live is more truly a universe of *spiritual realization* than is yours, because we have fewer hindrances along the way. We have fewer difficulties; we have fewer intrusions of matter, more spiritual dominance of power regarding mental reaction and spiritual enlightenment.

My spiritual sphere is really a realm, you could say, of instantaneous power in that the physical holding back is no longer there. We both use the same spiritual power, but you are limited in its use while I have almost no limitation. That, perhaps, is the greatest difference between our concepts of life—my understanding of life in a spiritual manner; your reception of life through a dense physical envelope, the physical body, and of course the limitations of your brain.

I'd like you to know that my own road is enmeshed with your world, in a manner of speaking—it is flowing through your world. It is entwined with physical substance, but not limited by it. You speak about going on a spiritual journey, such as you would make at the moment of death. Well, your spiritual journey doesn't take you anywhere because you will be living right where you are now, in the reality of spiritual being. The journey that you may think you take through death is only the journey of spiritual *enlargement* and *enfoldment*. We are all here together, infinite in time, limited in space, but infusing ourselves one to another through the infinitude of the eternal now.

I often sit in my room of meditation and try to receive from the Source a concept of the reality of all being. Of course that is impossible to do. Everything must be relative with our concepts because we are *of* God—but *not* God. We are seeking the Source; we are eternally finding ourselves unfolding and expanding with spiritual ideas and realization. Surely there must come a time when we will merge with that Source of our being, with the nirvana, the reality, truth, the light; but until that time we must express ourselves in our own way, in our own plane of existence, in the best manner possible.

I'd like to make this little talk a message of understanding on your plane so that you can realize the way it works in your everyday living. Realize that in your physical existence it is possible for you, through the power of choice, through your right to say yes or no, to have the privilege of cutting yourself off from the source of supply. That is, if you choose to do so, you can limit yourself unduly. You can expand your consciousness of life—just as surely as you can limit yourself through your choices—by choosing to recognize spiritual values.

I know you can be overcome with the turmoil of your existence on the earth plane, held back by the confusion and doubtfulness of decision. You can pause and await higher spiritual inspiration, or you can turn your face earthward and blunder your way through the darkness of physical concepts or choices. We recognize over here that there are many aspects of thinking and many avenues of expression.

There are limitless choices that you can make regarding the living of your life on the earth plane. If you choose, you can concentrate your thoughts upon material living. You can set yourself a goal toward perhaps making money, earning enough that you may have an existence which is free and easy and, with that, you may also express yourself spiritually. You could learn to live according to laws of spiritual understanding, enlarging your capacity for expressing life. That's the path I would have you choose, Riblet, the path of living in the world, of the world, with the world, expressing yourself entirely as you would in a normal manner. Then, in meditation you could become quiet, and, turning inward, you could receive inspiration from the Source and from the help which we are able to give you.

When you become quiet, spiritually, and ask prayerfully for aid from the spiritual Source, you have tapped the very source of your power of being. You can draw unto yourself unlimited power, unlimited vitality, unlimited reality of being. Set aside time for your meditation and glean from these powers of light some filtering-through of inspirational thought, such as you being a child of God, living directly from the Source. Then you can bring that power, that understanding, that realization, back to yourself in physical living, and express it to those about you.

Remember that your contact with the spirit world is a practical thing. It can enhance the power of living and can heighten your happiness. We are always happy to guide you in any manner that you may choose to allow us, but we will not intrude ourselves upon you. We only follow the way that you ask us to come and aid you.

I hope these few words have had some significance to you. Remember, Riblet, you are a spiritual being, living in a spiritual universe here and now. Your journey through death will not take you anywhere except to greater understanding of your attunement to the Source.

Reality

RIBLET: This is Saturday morning, and I've been reading and meditating. George has mentioned reality from time to time, and I feel he might like to expand on this subject this morning. . . .

GEORGE: And good morning, Riblet. It's good to be with you again. . . .

Have you ever stopped to think that the reality of life—the real world—is the spirit world—that souls are often close to the earth plane, but are *always* close just before they enter the earth plane at birth? So, the spirit world is the world whence cometh all humanity. You live in the physical plane for a few years. You die. You return to the spirit world from whence you came. . . . Looking at life from your viewpoint, you seem to think that physical living is the primary, definite reality of existence. I say, from the experience of my world, that my world is the real one, and your world—with the fewer vibrations of existence as you experience them through your physical senses—can only be an intrusion into the world of spirit. That is to say, the world of spirit is the *real* world.

The physical plane is just a little shelf on the infinitude of being. During the time you are incarnate in a physical body, expressing life in a limited manner through your physical senses, you should comprehend that this is always for your own betterment. Experiences you gain are those that relate to the soul. The memories you have, you carry with you. The experiences you undergo become a part of the growth of the spiritual be*ing* of you. And the *I am* of you, the soul of you, the greater self, is that part which assimilates these experiences and utilizes them in a manner that you can scarcely comprehend now.

Well, I didn't learn all this [with a chuckle] grand piece of philosophy in one chunk. I learned most of it very gradually as I tried to understand experiences over here as I relate them to you. I had to come back here to this world to understand some of the things that I underwent when I lived in your world, and now that I have been able to glimpse life from both sides, I have perhaps a fuller concept of reality than you have.

Perhaps I'm going a bit beyond your comprehension in the ideas I'm trying to foster right now. Suffice it to say that those experiences that are with you will come along in spite of you, or with your help. How the future happenings may stack up for you, or fall down before you, will depend on your reaction to the experiences you face.

The spirit people that you are working with are real, just as actual as are your friends on the physical plane. Oh, that you could comprehend the reality of my world, the actuality of me, George Felbers, as a person. I'm here, right at your bed, talking to you. We utilize the form of the body, be it spiritual, just as yours is physical. We have thoughts and comprehension and values. We term our experiences "realities" from the realm of thought. We utilize thought force as the reality of our being, knowing that it is within our power to mold our desires into actualities, utilize them—and then cast them into oblivion with a new thought and a new trend which makes a chain of reality as we attract new things to us.

You utilize thought in much the same manner except that the thought forces you use must work through a denser atmosphere, just as though you were living in a fog, a denseness, or a haze constantly surrounding you. All of these things that you want to do, or wish to maintain, or try to actualize, are the things which come to you dimly. You visualize gropingly, you miscomprehend the sharpness of detail and the reality of the forces as they react upon your consciousness. But you're doing well with these things, with the help of those of us over here, because we see a bit more clearly through this haze of material living. We are able to aid you in brightening your landscape, bringing to you more vivid coloration of the reality of existence. We can help you comprehend the chain of life as it goes on, even after you die, just as life goes on from day to day, as you experience it on the physical plane of life.

While you can see only the effects of the power of thought, you should recognize that the world of thinking, the mental realm, is a vast field of spiritual force that has *power*, real power. And you can do a great deal through selecting your thoughts, through projecting your thoughts out into the ether to anticipate, with emotion, those things which you can think into being. This may be through visualization, through mantras, through realizing the power of thoughts, or through repetitions of phrases which will be good to remind you of the things which you can project.

Those phrases you use—like, "I take my body, my mind, and my spirit and place them in the Light of God"—are a great force of good. You have no idea how the brilliance of the light begins to shimmer and glow about you when you utter those words with feeling and with a realization of attunement to our world! It has vitality, that phrase. It has life of itself, and when you speak those words over and over, you are fulfilling a law of God in that like attracts like and the power of light overcomes the power of darkness. These are laws of spiritual reality which you should recognize more and work with more consciously. . . .

Now we come to the truth of reality, as it is related to fantasy. The images that appear before you—both when you have your eyes closed and when you are awake and walking and active in your work—are incidences that will definitely show you the connection that you have made between your world and mine. There is no breaking of the chain, so that there is only the continuation of life as it is in reality, both for you and for me.

I want you to know, too, dear Riblet, that the inner you is greater than you can comprehend, and the work I am doing—as I continue to hold myself down in the astral plane close to the physical, so as to manifest more clearly and effectively for you—is a note of reality. You must consider this because the great ones speak through me to you, in a manner which you might not comprehend, but which you can intuitively realize and recognize as that which really is death and life. Positives and negatives—realities of the physical and images of the spiritual—all coalesce and become one and they are of the Father. The Father, as you know, is the Universal Whole, the Spiritual Power, which unites the universe.

This is George speaking. Good night.

Among the many things George discussed above, he touched upon the actual moment of transition from one world to the next. "Your spiritual journey," he said, "doesn't take you anywhere because you will be living right where you are now, in the reality of spiritual being. The journey that you may think you take through death is only the journey of spiritual *enlargement* and *enfoldment*." In the next message,

George addresses the topic directly and explains more specifically what happens to physical beings when we die and make the transition from the physical to the spiritual world.

In our Western culture, as a whole, death has been something to fear. In this message, George goes a long way to dispelling that fear. He presents a picture of purgatory that differs significantly from the teachings of many of our most influential religions, and points out that at death physical beings will find themselves "born again" into a spiritual realm that is harmonious with their present state of spiritual evolution. Their needs will be fulfilled; spirit teachers will be there to guide them.

Transition

RIBLET: This is Sunday morning, about eleven o'clock. I have been wondering about everything concerning life after death and the reality of going on.

GEORGE: I have come to you because of your request and will tell you about transition to the spirit world when you die, but be aware that life goes on unchanged when you pass away from the physical body.

There are several planes of life that exist which are lower in vibration rate than in this world where I live now. This plane of life and those worlds below me could be likened unto those which are called the purgatorial realms, or planes, of life. This is where the spirits that are newly born into the spirit world go where they may review their lives. They learn something of the spiritual evolution so they may cast off their previous activities, which were of the earth, and look toward spiritual light to guide them in future living. The purgatorial planes, or the lower realms of [spirit] life, are those planes to which most spirits go when they come over here to my world just at the time of death. They pass away from the physical body into a type of a sleep or a coma, and they awake in a strange place. It's like finding themselves in a different country, or perhaps a different environment which they'd never seen previously. The plane of life in which they find themselves is dependent upon their spiritual progress while they lived on your plane, on earth.

However, for you, Riblet, it will be a little different from that. You will enter a plane of life which will seem familiar to you, and you'll see those people around you whom you have seen many times before, both in spirit and on the physical plane. We want you to know that we are doing everything we can to help you make decisions whereby you can better "spiritualize" your life and let material things come for spiritual advancement.

The newly born spirits will progress according to their comprehension of spiritual life; and they will find themselves in a realm which is harmonious with their present evolutionary spiritual state. This place called purgatory is really a realm of life wherein you purge yourself of material aspects of living—the lesser, the negative things—and turn your face toward God, as it were, toward the higher spiritual realms. This is done with the aid of spirit teachers who are taught primarily to act as helpers in the darker planes. On those planes there are many structures that would be like hospitals or luxurious places of abode where newly born spirit people are taken to learn something about the laws governing their new existence.

These structures are placed in great park-like vistas where the landscape and the atmosphere is conducive to peace and quiet and to expansion of spiritual awareness. The light that will be shed onto these people in the way stations or houses of learning is such that gradually the newborn spirits will experience a newly awakened consciousness. They will begin to see that the ideas they had fostered through earth living, while real, were sometimes in error. They will be helped by guardians of light—those people who are trained in aiding the newborn spirits.

After they learn enough of the laws of life regarding spiritual living, they can advance into a new consciousness, a new vision, and different ideas. The next planes are devoted to inspirational living with progress in spirituality where the newly arrived spirits will live after death.

I think an important point to consider is the fact that, when you die, you are not going to be a so-called changed person. The realm of light will be close to you and about you if you can partake of it, if you can become consciously aware of it. It won't be there unless you can. The fulfillment of your needs will be at hand, and you can utilize those things which you need as soon as you learn the laws governing your future habitation. As I said, you will not be a changed person, as a spirit; you will go on exactly as you are now living on the earth plane.

The difference is that here, where I am, you will have divested yourself of your physical body. But still you will have a body, and it will be the exact duplicate or replica of you which is your spirit being. You will utilize this body for some time to come, for a long time perhaps, before a transition is made into another form of existence, which will go on beyond this realm in which I often find myself. The activities you will enjoy will depend a lot on the activities that you are having on the earth plane, that is, the activities of thinking, the activities of spiritual yearning.

If your thoughts, desires, and ideas tend to be harmoniously correct with the laws of spirit life, you will advance rapidly over here because you will find yourself uninhibited. You will not be thwarted by frustrating events which can hold you back from the true expression of your real self. However, those things will work themselves out in their own way and in their own manner without a great deal of manipulating on your part. You, when you are over here, will soon learn to live within the law of reality, just as you are living according to your understanding of reality there on the earth plane where you are now. You will be less inhibited, less limited, and more able to advance into higher realms of spiritual thinking. Over here, without the hesitancy of the brain, without the slower vibratory activity of physical manipulative thought, you will react intensely and quickly to things which will help control your existence in a much more harmonious way than you can possibly comprehend there where you are. I'm sure you need not worry too much about what's going to happen to you when you die. You'll be taken care of, just as you are taken care of there on the physical plane.

The laws of your existence in the physical plane state that you must live in certain lines of physical law in order to express life. For instance, in your world you must be in a place where there is sufficient oxygen to control the need of the oxygen in your physical body. You must live in a certain realm of light so that light rays may infiltrate themselves through your skin and into the cells of your body and give you energy from that source. You must be where there is sufficient food so that the body can break down certain substances and express life through the digestive process and in the cells of the physical body.

So it is over here. The things that you will do, reactions you will make, will be in line with spiritual law. Spiritual law governs here just as it does where you are except that here spiritual law is more readily attunable to one's needs. One thinks, and the law reacts with almost immediate, harmonious reaction. The law of cause and effect is quickened. Those things which you can utilize for your good are at hand, always to be had. You think you may struggle a bit over here or temporarily find yourself in a foreign environment, but you will progress rapidly because spiritual law is more amenable to spiritual thought and harmony—a truer law of life. Harmony will prevail here, where confusion and ignorance may be prevalent where you live.

Don't be confused as to those things which are in the Bible pertaining to life after death and the idea that man must be born again in order to inherit eternal life. We interpret "born again" to mean birth into the spirit world. Being born again means that you must reunite your spiritual thinking with true spiritual law. Then, you can move into the realm of spiritual life as it is over here—not as it is according to the concept of some people on the earth plane.

We are interested in your progress and observe the thoughts of yourself and those around you. We hope the time will soon come when we can find ourselves truly together. Perhaps I've utilized all the power that is available for me at this time, as words are coming distinctly but are slowing down in concept, so for the present, I'm going to withdraw and let you seek inspiration through meditation, through trying to receive the radiation of light as it comes to you from our world just now.

Riblet, I like to see nature at its best. I like to find my world of peace and quiet and relaxation and subdued light, and visualize the world about me as being the perfect place of nature—quiet, undisturbed, with sunlight filtering through the trees, sitting upon the edge of an infinite power of light as I would cast my eyes out toward the sea, surrounded only by the peace of the infinite, like the setting of the sun, like the waves upon water, like the peace such as would be suggested by a vision of a perfect blossom, a rose perhaps. . . . Amen

George speaking. Glad to have spoken. Will be with you very soon again. Bye.

Profound as they were, everything contained in these messages would be experienced by Riblet in a pair of "heavenly" out-of-body journeys.

chapter 13

HEAVENLY JOURNEYS

The two out-of-body experiences presented in this chapter, both of which took place when Rib was in his thirties, were ones in which he was offered a glimpse of the "heaven" that awaited him after death. In the first, he was privileged to see George's laboratory, a wondrous place where he was shown an instrument that George used to communicate with him. The highlight of this trip is a soaring flight to an even higher plane that left Rib awestruck. There, he saw beings of a very high order, and, finally, found himself before the ultimate teacher. And, he brought back one word that had seared itself into his very soul.

George's Astral Instrument and the Teacher

Today I went with George to his laboratory and saw the working of one of his astral instruments whereby he is able to know if his thought force is being rightly directed and received by me, as his receptor.

The instrument was in his circular study which was a beautiful room. The walls were entirely surrounded by books, the shelves reaching from floor to ceiling. In the center of the room, on a beautifully carved desk, sat this curious cage-like instrument. There were circular bands, horizontal and vertical, enclosing a ball-like beam of light which was capable of glowing brightly or of dulling into a soft red ember-like glow.

Through control knobs that were regulated from the desk, he was able to focus this beam of light into a short, sharp spark or ray. He showed me how he "tuned in" with me and was certain of results. First he made the necessary adjustments with the instruments and then he sat down near a window in a comfortable easy chair. I noticed that beams of a golden light poured in through the window, full on him, as he sat in his chair. Then, he explained, he focused his thoughts on the instrument and myself, and the stream of light became brighter and more dazzling. He asked me to make myself as passive as possible, and soon I became aware of a beautiful influence about me which I interpreted as a wave of primrose-colored light; this soon changed to a golden hue.

Then into my mind there were borne beautiful pictures of mountains and plains and trees. At this point I became lifted up, bodily it seemed—as I was then only utilizing my etheric body—and I seemed to soar out of this plane of life entirely, into a new dimension of time and space.

Here I was transplanted into a new life with a group of strangers and saw a crowd mingling together, speaking and gesticulating. Then I saw that these spiritual beings were differently clothed than were the other astral people I most frequently saw, and I became intuitively aware of the fact that I was among spiritual beings of a very high order. They were, each one, distinguished by the robes they were wearing. The robes were shown to me as radiant garments of light—predominant were deep blues and purples and the golden hue.

Before my startled gaze I saw the group gather into a circle and become silent and lost in meditation. Then, whereas before there had been no one in the center of the circle, now there appeared out of the invisible, the teacher of the group.

Here, words and memory fail me. The glory which was His still dazzles my mind when I think of Him, "The Teacher." He expressed All Perfection, All Beauty, All Peace. There was nothing but the perfection of Him and His attributes. As my sensitivity was quickened, I was both awed and inspired by Him who stood before us. And, from Him I learned the meaning of the thought, "Ultimate Perfection," for he personified the Living Ideal of that One like whom I most wish to be.

The beauty and majesty of His countenance and smile I cannot describe. The radiance and dazzling glory of His robes emitted a brilliance too startling for me to comprehend. The lessons He taught the group were far beyond my limited capacity to grasp. The meaning of the simple word "Life" as he used the word that day suggested realities that I cannot fathom with my limited understanding. But one clear, definite message I carried away with me, as a devotional thought which seared itself into my very soul, was the absolute glory of Reality which is somehow possible to attain—possible because of our inner-most, innate blendings of spirituality which unite us with the Source of our being.

This privilege, the knowledge of the limitless possibilities of man as God's own Son, must always henceforth be a bea-con-light for me to follow. This was the lesson learned. Thus was I privileged to see—Reality.

Then again, once more in the lesser actuality of my astral body, I found myself back in George's laboratory. George was still seated, unchanged, in his chair. I was still standing there near the instrument in the center of the circular room.

The light streaming in the window had changed to a pale, soft blue. I felt the lessening intensity of the force in the room. The curious cage-like instrument was still emitting a glow of light, only now it was not so intense. I felt the reaction to the contact with such cosmic beings and felt humble, awed, appreciably small in accomplishment in comparison with those I had seen.

Now George stirred, seemingly out of a reverie. He mo-tioned me closer to him, and I knew he meant we must return to my physical body. I knew I must consent to go, and yet it was with reluctance I would do so, for the enormous contrast of the physical body to the glories of the heaven plane was a fact I did not much want to face.

And yet—I knew. A drowsy, numbing sensation of falling down, down—back into my physical counterpart. A shudder of the entire physical body, a sensation as of a slight percussion or jolt, an opening of the eyes, and I was back on earth, in my study, ready to transcribe to paper these amazing actualities!

This is surely the most momentous astral projection that I've experienced, and I can't find words to describe the emotion I felt. Again, I'm humbled and will be eternally grateful to George for his help in this adventure.

After completing the exercise of writing down this experience in his journal, Riblet sat for a long time, attempting to digest this exhilarating experience. "It's a good thing I have this written down," he thought to himself, "because no one would believe me if I ever tried to tell them!" He relived the unique emotions he felt when on that higher plane—a place he was never to see again as long as he lived on the earth plane. He felt exceedingly humble as well as gratified, realizing again that he was indebted to George for arranging and helping him achieve this glorious trip.

The second out-of-body journey that I include in this chapter was a true social event. It came to be known as "The May Day Party" and I present it here, as we approach the end of Riblet's physical life, as it provides a beautiful and comforting view of what awaited Rib at the end of his earth life—and for that matter, what may await us all. It was also

Riblet's favorite out-of-body experience, perhaps because of its highly social aspect—Rib always loved a party!

To the delight of the audiences that gathered to hear him lecture at Camp Chesterfield and Lily Dale, he enjoyed reading the May Day experience from his journal, making remarks as he went along. And later in his life, when he learned that I was interested in astral projection, he provided me with this special May Day "lecture" by way of an audiotaped letter— a letter which I did not receive until after his death.

As he did with his camp audiences, in this audio letter to me, he read from the journal and commented as he went along. The letter, I believe, captures Riblet's curious and compassionate nature.

The May Day Party

Because I'm doing kind of an unprecedented thing, I scarcely know how to tell you about it before beginning. At the insistence of George—and it was sheer insistence—I dug into an old journal I had, wherein I had copied my experiences of astral projections.

You know, in years past when I was trying to establish a practice, I had time on my hands, having the entire upstairs of my father's house to myself where I could go and spend hours. That's when I did most of my work in astral projection—a long time ago.

After each experience, when I came back into the body after being out awhile, I would take the journal and write everything down. Now, George has impressed upon me the idea to read to you one of the experiences we had concerning what he calls a May Day party. Here's the way the "tale" goes, and this is the experience I had at that time.

You'd mentioned that astral projections interested you a lot, and in those years, I did that type of thing and kept a journal of my experiences. I look back now and realize some of the things that occurred I took for granted at the time, but which were evidently quite out of the ordinary.

Anyway, this is the experience, from the journal.

The day is cloudy but warm and balmy. Today I "got out" again. This time, a May Day visit to many of my friends in the etheric world.

I first placed myself in a comfortable position in an easy chair that I usually use for my experiences, in the locked study, and sat back for a few minutes of reverie and relaxation. I was thinking of my friends over there and longing with a deep emotion to somehow break through again and to glimpse once more the reality of the things as they were with these folks. So, I sat back resting, my eyes closed in this comfortable chair, and George appeared instantly at my side, just as soon as I had relaxed and had begun to breathe deeply and rhythmically.

He asked whether or not I would be willing to go with him where he wanted to take me, and of course I acquiesced to this willingly. Simply and easily, and almost suddenly but nearly imperceptibly, I felt myself drawn out of my body, through my head, at the back of the neck.

This time I was surrounded by light—bright light—all about me, and a feeling of power, a feeling of energy, surging through everything. And this particular time, no force was needed to jerk me free from physical bonds.

Sometimes I had a little trouble getting away, but this time I just stepped away from the relaxed physical form and turned to view it for a brief moment. I always like to see the body quiet and resting and in a comfortable position, because it's uncomfortable when I come back, if the body hasn't been comfortable during the interval when I'm out.

And then I floated vertically and easily upward, out and away from that physical room. After a brief sensation of drifting upward, I found myself in a new but very natural environment. I seemed to be in a grove or park which extended as far as I could see. All was beauty, symmetry, and naturalness. Nature in perfection was what I seemed to sense as I stood there. And, then again, suddenly, I found myself in the center of a circle of trees; and I was sitting in a comfortable chair. Placed before me was a table covered with a dainty white cloth, which, evidently, was set for party refreshments. Well, George was there, seated opposite me and he was grinning in a very amiable, pleased manner.

You know, George himself is a *real* person, just as real to me as I am to myself, and he's individualistic in his approach to life and the things he does and the way he reacts to me; so I always respect the individuality of him. This time he was very amiable and pleased, and he sat just as though he was holding back a very happy secret from me.

I glanced about the park, which seemed endless to my poorly focused etheric vision.

You know, when you first get over there, that world needs focusing, just like the need to focus at times if your glasses don't fit well; things are a little blurry and you're not sure of your location, or how you'll react to things.

During that time as we were sitting there, George chatted nonchalantly to me, and then he finally said, "Well, today we are to have a little party over here. Arrangements have been made, and some old friends are invited. Please don't be surprised at whom you might see." And with this he waved his hand airily, pointing off into the distance.

He pointed toward a path that approached me on my right, and there, coming down the walk, I saw a group of figures, just as we would see figures approaching us from a distance here.

"You know, this is *my* day," George grinned, mischievously, "and so it's a May Day party for *you*, Kid."

That's another thing, too, that's strange. All through the years, as long as I've known George, he's called me "the kid." Any resemblance to being a kid [humorously] was removed years ago, but not so with George. So he said:

"It's a May Day party for you, Kid." And then I sat up and looked and watched the approaching spirits with interest. They came closer, and I was both elated and surprised when I recognized them. They were old, almost-forgotten friends from my old hometown. And they were coming up to greet me.

First to come down the path was a gentleman who had died, I believe, a year or two ago, and with him was his son, whom I knew not so well, and his wife, whom I had never met. "Don Council, do you know me?" I asked happily. "I never dreamed of meeting you *here.*"

You see, the immediate one that I would enjoy seeing was not the official greeter. Don had been a neighbor in the town where I grew up, and I had known him quite well, but had lost track of him through the years. I knew of his death and had only casually gotten in touch with his family since that time.

Don said, "I knew you were coming, and I brought along my son, whom you know, and my wife, whom you didn't know. I realized, too," he hastily added, "that you are with us for a short time only, for you are yet earth-fastened."

That was a term that interested me, and he informed me,

"So I won't take up too much of your time. Here are some others that perhaps you'd rather talk to than us." And, turning, he made a little motion to the two ladies coming up the path at my side. Well, I turned and joyously met my grandmother Riblet, gone over about two years earlier, and with her was her friend whom she knew prior to her passing. This friend and neighbor had made *her* transition just a short time before my grandmother.

There's a very interesting psychic incident connected with their transitions. For several days before Grandmother died, she lay in a coma. This neighbor, Mrs. Shoemaker, lived alone next door. She fell in her kitchen, broke her hip and died, and no one found her for several days. All this time my grandmother had been in a coma, and *after* Mrs. Shoemaker's funeral and burial, Grandmother woke and said, "You know, I've had the nicest chat with Mrs. Shoemaker, and wasn't it a shame she had to be all alone when she died?" Shortly after that, my grandmother died.

Glad was my greeting and happy was I with this brief welcome on this day, to those in the other world. How good it was to greet all of those good home folks, and how fine it was that I could go in freedom, in my own etheric body, to such a glorious spiritual reunion. I wanted badly to tell them that this time I was there to stay; but I knew such was not the fact, so I could only tell them I was there for a short time and would see them again.

My extreme happiness to greet them there at all, even if it was such a short time, pleased me greatly. And George, I saw, was enjoying all this immensely, because I knew I was his especial charge this day, and I gave him a word of grateful acknowledgment for the privilege of being there with him.

Now, the others, seemingly with one accord, fell back, away from me a few steps, and I felt a quickening of the spiritual atmosphere. And in this peaceful, quiet setting, my glance instinctively took me down to the path, toward which all of the others were looking, and there coming radiantly toward me in all the beauty of her true etheric presence, walked my arisen mother. Toward her I sprang with outstretched arms and such a joyous reunion took place there. Time and difference and spheres of activity of life and death were forgotten. My being fully blended with hers, and this moment seemed the supreme happiness of my existence. It was a reunion once again of souls through love which the barriers of death could not separate, a triumph of spirit, as side by side we stood there, reunited. She was in all the glory of her majestic spirit body, free and attuned to the plane of life upon which she was living after her release from the physical through death, and I, in my immature etheric presence, incapable of expressing myself independently.

I was there with George's help and only freed from my physical prison house temporarily, because of spiritual laws partially conquering misunderstood natural obstacles. Thus we were together for a time, reunited on one plane of life. There were my friends and loved ones, gone to the fourth dimension, through death, and here also was I, able to function there for a limited time, and in a very feeble manner. But notwithstanding all these barriers, the reunion of spirit was made!

Now my mother greeted the assembled friends, and together we sat and chatted. During the course of our conversation, Mother relayed to me some interesting information. "I have a note with me," she said, "from one of your newer etheric friends," and she handed me what might be the etheric counterpart of a short letter. I glanced at the words and read the signature. It was from Edmund Hanson, a friend whom I have come to know through his family, left here on the earth plane.

"I have met Edmund," continued Mother, "and although he could not be present with us today, he did want me to hand you this." I glanced through the note. These were the words he had written: "To my new-found earth friend: Greetings and a welcome from those of us over here who can make contact with you. Please accept my words of appreciation. Thank you for what you have done for my family. I am closer than they know. My guardianship is continuous, even after death. But I did not know it at the time, when I came over. Thanks for all of your help and attention to Ben [Edmund's son, whom Riblet had taken an interest in after Edmund's death]. We'll see him through. Edmund."

Of course this personal note touched me deeply. I was grateful for the knowledge that I had, so that I could continue to help. Truly, this May party was a rare treat, indeed; but I knew that the time of my departure was drawing near.

George arose and stood by my side, signaling me to make my adieus. I greeted all my assembled friends and then allowed the pull of the earth to take me here.

I made this observation on returning: When I commenced to leave my beloved mother and friends on the etheric plane, I know their reaction to my going was that I was simply and definitely fading from their etheric sight, such as ice might melt in the bright sunlight. I simply and slowly grew indistinct and then finally became invisible. This is the same reaction in reverse as when we "tune in" to spirit entities.

George explains it deftly by applying it as a definite change of vibrational activity. My personal reaction was that I simply felt a pull back to the physical body again. It was too strong to resist. So what can I say other than to state that I was pulled obliquely downward, out of the etheric realm, which exists somewhere in space, back through the walls into the confines of my physical study. There, as the pull to the body became stronger and less easily governed, I suddenly stiffened in my astral form, assuming a position parallel to and immediately above the physical counterpart, and I simply "dropped into it."

The re-association of the two vehicles occasioned a slight jolt, almost as though I had fallen a foot or two. A sharp, sudden intake of breath, a wave of involuntary spasmodic contraction, and I was back in the physical again.

I glanced up and saw George wave a cheery goodbye, and he, in turn, vanished from my physical sight.

That's just one of the experiences, Betti, that I've had, which tells me of the continuity of life and the reality of things beyond the physical.

If these words will do anyone any good toward easing this passage from death into life, eternal life, feel free to utilize this experience of mine all you care to.

Perhaps the reason the May Day out-of-body experience was so popular with Riblet's audiences had to do with the images that many people hope for after death. The components were all there: a reunion with family and friends, all happy, attractive, in perfect health. The setting was in a beautiful park—"nature in perfection," as Rib put it. This social affair brought joy to all who were there, and to the audiences who experienced it vicariously through Riblet's telling of it, myself included.

chapter 14

RIBLET'S TRANSITION

Riblet's transition to the other side took place when he was in his seventies. For some time it had been obvious that the physical symptoms he had been experiencing called for medical attention, but he procrastinated as long as he could. He finally went to a physician in Florida, where he was living at the time, and was told that surgery was necessary. Agreeing to the procedure, Riblet got along pretty well for several months. When he returned to his home in Goshen, he visited his own doctor. After undergoing various tests and x-rays, he was told he didn't have long to live. I'm sure at this point he wasn't surprised, but relieved, ready to relinquish the physical body for a new, healthy one.

Perhaps because he realized he would soon be with the loved ones he had visited on the spirit plane many times before, he complained about his illness only occasionally. And while he tended to be withdrawn as he approached his final days, overall he seemed to be accepting of his death.

Mother, who was seventy-nine at the time, had come up from her home in Florida to be with Riblet. I was at home in Pennsylvania. I didn't know his precise condition but had decided if I had to make a choice, I would rather visit him while he was living—a much more meaningful experience—than wait and attend his funeral. So, I went to join Mother.

Rib was in the hospital when I got there, but it was decided the next day that he could be discharged to our care. Charles offered his home and a hospital bed was brought in.

After getting Riblet settled in, and while I was watching over him, I thought about the life he had led, and this final illness, remembering our conversation on the beach, a year or so before, when he had said he wished he could pass over sooner rather than later; he felt he could continue his work on the other side. As a fatalist, he had always expressed his opinion about birth and death. "There's a time to be born and a time to die," he would say. I presume he had these thoughts during the remainder of his life.

When I considered Rib's present lingering illness and compared it to the circumstances of other people I had known, particularly those who had died suddenly, I had an insight: I understood that it isn't necessary to be sick in order to make the transition from the physical to the spirit world. I wondered if Rib might have thought about this. Perhaps. What were his beliefs? I don't know. There was no question, however, but that he looked forward to the passage.

Over the years, George's messages to Riblet had contained explanations of the transition experienced by newly born spirits. Those whose spiritual progress on earth wasn't significant, George had explained, would need to be assigned, at the time of transition, to a place or a plane where spirit teachers would be able to help them. But, he said to Rib, "*You* will enter a plane of life which will seem familiar to you, seeing those people whom you have seen frequently in your out-of-body trips."

During this time, Rib received a loving, hand-written letter from one of his patients, expressing beautifully what many felt for him:

> Goshen, Indiana
> June 19, 1978
>
> Dear Dr. Hout,
>
> If only we could help you as you've helped hundreds of us. "Us" are those who sought you out for help with maladies that no one else seemed to recognize. You had a God-given touch that somehow steered you to the source of a malady. Then you would attack it as though it were the devil itself. Invariably—and I mean without exception—you helped us.
>
> I am grieved that you are seriously ill and there is not another Dr. Hout to ameliorate your illness. I entreat the Source of all existence, the Source being the Infinite One in whom we both believe.

Why not? Why not help for the man who me-
diated a service of good to humanity? I am assured
that God is with you . . . and so is my love,

V. P.

I wondered if Rib was indeed visiting on the other side
during this time, as, for the most part, he spoke only when
spoken to during those days.

After caring for him, at Charles's home, for about two
weeks, it was impossible to predict how long he would last,
and I needed to return to Pennsylvania. So, I made my plans
to fly home. When I told Rib I had to leave, he expressed his
deep appreciation for the care I had given him. At our last
meeting, I took his hand in mine and said, "We've had a lot
of good times, Rib, I love you." He looked at me and replied,
"We'll always have good times, Bett." We both knew this was
the final goodbye and I left. I can't say I was deeply upset because I knew for a certainty that he was, indeed, going to a
better place. I was comfortable with his expected transition,
and none of us present gave a thought to providing heroic
means to keep him alive.

When I arrived at home, I kept in close touch by
phone. The following day, it was decided that, without me
there to nurse him, Rib would be better cared for in a nursing facility. Apparently he was semiconscious during the
short ambulance trip and in less than twenty-four hours it
was obvious that the end was near. My older brother, my
mother, and Charles were in attendance. Finally, Charles

said gently to his friend, "Why don't you let go, Rib?" Shortly after, the family stepped out to let a nurse check and turn him. And with my brother waiting by the door, expecting to be with Rib when he passed, the nurse came out and told him that Riblet was gone.

Rib's funeral was traditional, with a modest crowd, many of his friends, family, and patients having already made the transition themselves. What was remembered by those who knew him best was that he had helped countless people in his lifetime. His principal legacy is simply this: His life experiences, his miraculous healing ability, his contacts with those who had passed on before him, all provide hope and guidance to those of us on this earth plane. His experiences can help us live better lives now, alleviate our fears of death, and comfort and guide us at our time of transition.

In an undated poem I found among his papers, Rib expressed his deeply held belief about a Higher Power. I will leave you with his words—

Father
As a bent reed I come to Thee
Helpless and forlorn;
Without Thy help
I would be naught.

For Thou art me
And in me
And through me
And beyond me,
And I am Thine!

Infinite Eternity rolls about me
Could I but know and yet I *do* know
Deep within.

Naught need I do
But know Thee better,
For naught there is
But Thee!

Would I but take time
To live my awareness
Of Thee!

I can do naught
But love Thee, Father—
For I am Thine.

appendix 1

OSTEOPATHY

Osteopathic medicine is a distinct form of American medical care that was developed in 1874 by Andrew Taylor Still, M.D. Dissatisfied with nineteenth-century medical practices, particularly with what he saw as the misuse of drugs common to the day, Dr. Still set himself apart from his peers and was one of the first to study the attributes of good health in order to better understand the disease process. In fact, he pioneered the idea of "wellness." And today, osteopaths are trained to treat "the whole person" rather than the specific symptom or illness.

According to the American Osteopathic Association (AOA), osteopathic medicine is a philosophy of health care and a distinctive art supported by expanding scientific knowledge. Its philosophy embraces the concept of the unity of the living organism's structure and function (anatomy and physiology).

Osteopathic concepts emphasize the following principles: 1) The human being is a dynamic unit of function; 2) The body possesses self-regulatory mechanisms which are self-healing in nature; 3) Structure and function are interrelated at all levels; 4) Rational treatment is based on these principles.

In today's terms, each patient's particular health risks are evaluated and the osteopathic physician acts as a teacher, helping the patient change unhealthy patterns and thereby take more responsibility for their own well-being.

There are nineteen osteopathic medical colleges scattered across the United States. Over half of all Doctors of Osteopathy (D.O.s) practice in primary care areas such as pediatrics, general practice, obstetrics/gynecology, and internal medicine. Others practice in specialties such as surgery, psychiatry, and orthopedics. D.O.s receive extra training in the musculoskeletal system, the interconnected system of nerves, muscles, and bones that make up two-thirds of our body mass. Knowledge of the musculoskeletal system is used in osteopathic manipulative treatment (known as OMTs), a hands-on treatment in which the D.O. applies force to the body's affected area, to treat what they call structural abnormalities. They then apply "specific corrective forces to relieve joint restrictions and misalignments."

Sports medicine is a natural outgrowth of osteopathic practice because of its focus on the musculoskeletal system, osteopathic manipulative treatment, as well as diet, exercise, and fitness. In fact, many sports-team physicians are D.O.s.

For more information, contact the American Osteopathic Association, 142 E. Ontario Street, Chicago, Illinois 60611, (800) 621-1773. Or visit their website at www.aoa.org.

appendix 2

MATERIALIZATION

"The term materialization," writes A. Campbell Holms in *The Facts of Psychic Science and Philosophy*,[1]

> usually refers to the temporary creation of a living human body, in whole or in part, apparently out of nothing, which is vitalized and controlled by a spirit. The phenomenon is, without a doubt, the most impressive and significant of all spiritual manifestations. A perfect materialization requires special power in the medium and it can only be accomplished under suitable conditions and after long practice.

When asked about materialization, Rib's response was,

> It's almost like a fog, a milky fog, and often it comes like waves. This is the growing of ectoplasm from

the auras and etheric bodies of the sitters [those present at a séance], and if anyone in the room—a medium—has a particular chemistry which would allow it to be utilized, that's the way materializations occur.

The word *ectoplasm* was coined in the nineteenth century by the French physiologist, Dr. Charles Richet, a psychic researcher and author. Sir Arthur Conan Doyle, in volume 1 of *The History of Spiritualism*,[2] goes into great detail about his own and others' experiences in this field, as well as the scientific studies that were being conducted during his lifetime. It was Doyle's belief that in the future a new, separate science would be formed to study ectoplasm, but this "new science" never came to pass. Rib, at one point, explained why he felt this was so:

> The phenomena of physical mediumship, with the occurrence and production of ectoplasm is going out more all the time. . . . Spiritualism was born in a day when there was great materialism and there was a need to call attention to the movement. The physical phenomena are actually dying away. It's served its purpose.

It's interesting to note that in Doyle's writing there is ongoing commentary regarding the various tests, witness statements, and investigations that were conducted to satisfy skeptical readers who might otherwise dismiss this type of psychic phenomena as poppycock. And, in *The Facts of Psychic Science*, Holms presents four chapters on materialization, with descriptions of the steps that were taken by serious investigators to show that the demonstrations were genuine.

In the various studies and eyewitness accounts, ectoplasm has been described in many ways—as white, black, gray, or even flesh colored, and sometimes as translucent. "Often it appeared first as a white mist," Holms writes. "One moment it might be like paste in a state of flux and a moment later extended like muslin. Some experimenters asserted that it had an ozone-like odor. Sometimes it emerged like thick paint out of a tube, and continued to flow outward with a leaping movement." One person described it as gelatinous; another compared it to an umbilical cord.

According to the studies conducted, ectoplasm is believed to come from the medium's body. In some cases, it seemed that fine threads were being drawn out from the pores of the skin. In other cases, it was reported that a filmy, cloudy patch of something white was observed on the floor in front of the "cabinet," an enclosed, curtained-off space where the medium would sit, the belief being that a confined space is necessary to contain the psychic energy. On occasion, materialized spirits were reported to open the curtain, step out, and walk toward the sitters. The ectoplasm seemed to flow out onto the floor from underneath the curtain, gradually expanding, visibly extending, lying and moving, fold upon fold. It has also been said to ooze from the medium, through the mouth and other orifices, as well as from the whole body. Many older books and spiritualist newspapers contain photographs of these occurrences.

In some reports, the material has been said to rise slowly near the center of the mass, as if a figure were underneath it, and a hand, or arm, or perhaps a head form. In some cases, whole human figures have been said to appear, and are then most often recognized by one of the sitters. More recent psychics have reported similar experiences. In the 1970s, psychic Jane Roberts described her own experience with ectoplasm and reported having materialized extra fingers during a séance.[3]

Not surprisingly, such séances seem to be most successful when the sitters are accepting of the demonstration, less so when they are skeptical, suspicious of failure or trickery. In other words, it seems that each of the sitters contributes to the power that produces the ectoplasm used by spirits to form the figures that the sitters then see and interact with.

Over the years, Rib experienced several materializations, one being that of his grandfather, as described in chapter 1, another being especially significant to me as it involved Rib's mother—my beloved grandmother—who had passed to the other side a few years earlier. Rib first told my brother Dick about the incident in the 1970s, but this detailed report came, after Rib's passing, from his friend Charles, who was present at the séance and tape recorded his account of the episode—

The Materialization of Riblet's Mother

The room in which the event took place was in a basement with cement block walls and a concrete floor that accommodated fifteen or twenty people. In this work a dim red light is used, just enough for the sitters to see the materialized forms. The medium sat behind the cabinet, which was a curtain drawn across one corner of the room. She sat in there on a straight chair, with the red light at the opposite corner of the room, hanging down from the ceiling. She went into a deep trance. When the spirits walked out of that cabinet, they pulled the curtain aside and you could see her sitting there. All around her was that ectoplasm. It looked like dense fog, and it moved; you could see it moving.

These fully clothed forms walked out into the room, and they called up individuals they wanted to talk to. Rib's mother came out, and she called him up. She walked clear into the center of the room, a number of feet away from the cabinet, and he went to her. Then she called me up. We shook hands, and her hand felt solid. There wasn't any clammy feeling to it at all. The only thing was that the whole appearance of the form had kind of a waxy appearance, not quite like solid flesh, like we're accustomed to feeling and seeing. She talked a few minutes to Rib and me, and even kissed him on the forehead, I remember. These spirits can only stay out there so long, and the power begins to wane, and then the form begins to disintegrate. She said, "Now I have to go." There were a few of the forms that went back into the cabinet, but most of them just started melting down through the floor, and as each form hit the floor, it just disappeared. She talked, as did most of the others, until her chin hit the floor! This group of sitters were all receptive to the materialization and this no doubt contributed to the success of the evening.

appendix 3

RESCUE CIRCLES

As related in chapter 8, Rib had some experience, while out-of-body, with helping a newly born spirit accept and adjust to the fact that he had indeed "died" and made the transition to the spirit world. But as Rib didn't address the issue at length anywhere in his journal or recordings, I thought readers might be interested in my own, albeit limited, knowledge and experience with rescue circles.

In 1981 I attended a workshop at the Robert Monroe Institute in Virginia. As I learned, the goal of a rescue circle is to guide wayward souls who do not realize they are dead into understanding and accepting their situation and helping them to move on to the higher planes. It seems that spirit teachers are unable to reach these newly transitioned spirits, one reason being that some of them are simply ignorant of the existence of the spirit world and therefore unable to receive the help offered.

The rescue circle consists, ideally, of a medium, and a knowledgeable, compassionate, and articulate person able to counsel the distressed spirit speaking through the medium. At the workshop I attended, we listened to an audiotape of Robert Monroe's work in a rescue circle. In this particular case, the counselor was Monroe himself, founder of the institute, and author of the groundbreaking and definitive book on out-of-body experiences, *Journeys Out of the Body*.[1]

The voice that came through the medium during this rescue-circle session was a long-suffering sailor, apparently the only survivor of a long-ago shipwreck. He had died many decades previously, but was mentally trapped in cold ocean water, trying to stay afloat. He called for help, saying over and over that he was very cold and wanted to be saved from his terrible fate. At first he was talking so much he couldn't hear Mr. Monroe calling to him and telling him repeatedly that he had died and was now a spirit.

Finally, the sailor listened to what he was being instructed to do, which was to call for his mother or other family member with whom he had been close. Before long the young man was amazed to see, above his head, first a hand and then an arm, and he held up his own hand to grasp it. He was soon out of the water and reunited with his mother and family, thanking Mr. Monroe for his rescue.

Listening to this tape was indeed a poignant and impressive experience.

In research conducted much earlier than that of Robert Monroe, a California doctor, Carl A. Wickland, and his wife, a medium, experimented in this field. Dr. Wickland's particular interest was in normal and abnormal psychology.

His book, *Thirty Years Among the Dead*,[2] published in 1924, contains helpful and interesting information, with chapters on Christian Science, suicide, materialism, and many other subjects. It also contains many word-for-word interviews with dozens of spirit people who were often brought forward by spirit teachers for counseling. Often, these rescued spirits came back at a later date to thank the couple for their help.

In one particularly interesting account from *Thirty Years Among the Dead*, the author tells of a particular spirit's experience of learning that he had died. He was identified as Mr. M. He had very recently passed over and had been acquainted with Dr. Wickland. When Mr. M. spoke through Mrs. Wickland, the doctor asked who he was. "I thought it strange that he did not know me," Mr. M. replied, "but I told him I was Mr. M. and asked whether he did not know me. The doctor was very much surprised and explained as gently as he could that I had passed out of my mortal body a week before and was now a spirit. That was the first time I realized that I had passed out of my physical body." Shortly afterward the spirit's mother, father, sister, brother, and other relatives and friends joined him for a happy reunion. Later he remarked that in the physical world, "life is only a school where we gain understanding through experience. In the spirit world we go on and on, progressing, but before we can progress, we must have understanding of the spiritual laws."

On a more personal note, my own mother had not at first realized that she had passed to the other side. Mother, who was ninety-one and living in a nearby nursing home when she died, was in a semiconscious condition for several days prior to passing over. A few weeks after her memorial, I went for a reading to my good friend and favorite psychic, Amy Bortner, of Philadelphia. I asked about my mother and was told by Amy's guides that she was doing well and adjusting, but that when she had become conscious in the facility on the other side, she had not realized that she had died. (I must digress to point out that it was at my mother's knee I learned of the spirit world and life after death.) The caretakers on the other side asked my mother, "Well, don't you notice a difference from the place and the nurses where you *were* and the place where you are now?" She replied that she just felt she had been transferred to another nursing home, or something like that. I was told that it took several such conversations before she was satisfied that she had indeed left her earth body.

My mother's passing had taken place in the early morning hours, and because I was not notified about her impending death, I was not present when it occurred. And so I was comforted to know that her transition had been so smooth.

appendix 4

A MODEL TRANSITION

My brother Dick was in his early forties when he was diagnosed with pancreatic cancer. Through four medical crises he survived when there was no reason to expect him to live more than a few days—or even hours. But he "fooled" everyone, and in the large Midwestern hospital where he was treated, he came to be known as the "miracle man." After six grueling months in the intensive care unit, he went home to recuperate. And with the support of his wife, who is a nurse, his three children, and extended family and friends, he gradually regained his strength. My mother felt that his life had been extended for a special reason.

Eventually, he got to the point where, for about ten months, he was able to go back to work as a telephone installer. But then metastasis of his pancreatic cancer reappeared, and a minor operation substantiated the surgeon's suspicion that the malignancy was widespread and, in fact, terminal. The doctor advised Dick not to undergo chemotherapy or return to work.

Quite naturally, Dick experienced anger and marked depression at this turn of events, but perhaps because of the help and support of his family and friends, he passed through these stages in only a week or two. He called me the morning he was to leave the hospital for the second time and said, "I've got my head screwed on straight now, and I'm anxious to get home." He sounded so good. He had faced his approaching transition, reached peaceful acceptance, and desperately wanted to live out the remainder of his life at home. (The hospice movement wasn't widespread at that time, but what he desired is now referred to as hospice care.)

And so it was that my brother became a model dying patient. In fact, it was this "teaching capacity" that our mother referred to when she had said that she felt Dick's life was extended for a very special reason.

Dick took on his new role almost with vigor. For one thing, he hoped to spare his wife, children, and others close to him as much anguish as possible at the time of his passing. They had been completely supportive through his critical six-month illness and were just as supportive now that he was known to be terminally ill.

Fortunately, he was up and about and able to participate in family activities to a considerable extent after coming home. And he rightly reasoned that if he made all the necessary decisions about his funeral beforehand, at the time of his death his wife would be spared a significant amount of the anxiety of decision making. He worked with his minister, the mortician, and the cemetery representative, as well as his wife and children, and another family with whom he was close. He included them all, to the extent that they were willing and able to participate.

In planning his final ceremony, this gentle man first decided on the clothes he would be dressed in. Then one of his children and his godchildren, with whom he was very close, accompanied him to the funeral home to pick out the casket. Dick decided on a hand-polished wooden coffin that featured a gold-colored lining. His godson told our mother that this choice related to the fact that the wood was hand-crafted. Later, at the time of the funeral, the boy fingered the beautiful wood surface, repeating the movements of the craftsman's hands.

Dick wanted a celebration of his *life* rather than his death. Organ music, he felt, was too somber, so he requested that a particular Ernie Ford record of hymns be played; and they were. He requested that mourners not wear dark clothing, and he insisted that the minister wear a sport coat rather than a suit or ministerial robe. He even went so far as to instruct the minister to say that while he hadn't chosen to die in his mid-forties, leaving his wife and children to fend for themselves, he had no fear of the coming experience—he felt that he would simply pass through a door and go on living in another country. The minister agreed that Dick's philosophy of life—and death—was beautiful to behold. The mortician said, "In my thirty years of experience in funeral work, I have never before met a person as remarkable as this man was in regard to his own death."

Dick's wife was indeed greatly relieved when the time came to make funeral arrangements. "He knew what he wanted and set his own limit on spending," she said. "This way I was assured it was exactly as he had chosen." (How many times have we heard of families choosing inordinately expensive funerals that they could ill afford?)

Dick's entire family, myself included, felt that his funeral was truly a celebration of a life well spent. It wasn't that we didn't grieve, or that he wasn't missed by everyone who knew him, but with his effort in planning his own funeral, he taught a lesson about life to us all. What better way to teach children that death is a part of life and not a thing to be feared—that the ending of one life is the beginning of another?

Endnotes

Introduction

1. For more on my brother Dick's passing, and how he prepared for it, see appendix 4, "A Model Transition."

chapter 1

The Boy Who Was Different

1. For those readers interested in exploring information about the angelic kingdom, I would suggest two excellent books. In the first, *Fairies at Work and at Play*, author Geoffrey Hodson describes, as the title suggests, the fairies and other elementals that live and work among plants, grasses, and other living things (Wheaton, IL: Theosophical Publishing House, 1982). In *The Real World of Fairies: A First Person Account* (also published by the

Theosophical Publishing House, in 1977; second edition, 1999), author Dora Van Gelder, who claims she has the ability to see and converse with all manner of angelic beings, discusses how members of the angelic kingdom each have their particular duties and happily accept their assignments for the good of all.

2. According to Webster's Dictionary, "New Thought originated in 1887 and is a mental healing movement . . . devoted to spiritual healing and the creative power of constructive thinking."

In her article, "Defining New Thought in an Old Thought World" (*New Thought*, spring 1996, volume 80, no. 1, p. 8), Kathy Gottberg explains:

> Charles S. Braden [well known for his writings regarding New Thought] describes New Thought as neither a church, cult nor sect. It asks no allegiance to creeds, form or personality. . . . New Thought believes that the great need is not to be so much a theoretical Christianity as an applied one. It holds that all religions and all peoples are at different states of growth. . . . Under his definition, New Thought is positive, constructive, a philosophy of optimism; and of the recognition, realization, and manifesting of God in Man.
>
> New Thought supports the idea that we are much more than human beings that evolved to the point of self-conscious awareness. Instead, we are

individualized expressions of the One, who collectively have evolved this planet and our bodies and consciousness to the point where we are today.

3. Though never an official publication of the New Thought movement, *Nautilus* was probably the most widely read of the many New Thought publications of the time and was very influential. The magazine included articles on such subjects as psychology, travel, astronomy, scientific discovery, hypnotism, rhythmic breathing, telepathy, psychometry, clairvoyance, and auras.

Nautilus was the private enterprise of its editor, Elizabeth Towne, who was originally a Methodist before taking up New Thought and becoming a teacher. She founded the magazine in 1898 and continued its publication for more than fifty years. At the peak of its popularity *Nautilus* was distributed to 45,000 subscribers monthly. By its tenth year of publication, some two and a half million copies had been distributed. In 1953, Mrs. Towne, then of advancing years, discontinued publication.

4. The name was later changed to Kirksville College of Osteopathic Medicine.

5. See appendix 1, "Osteopathy," for more information.

6. *Wanderings of a Spiritualist* was originally published in London in 1921 (Hoden & Stoughton). The first American edition came out the same year (New York: George H. Doran) and a new edition was published in 1988 by Ronin Publishing.

chapter 3

A Picture of Life on the Other Side

1. The aunts were sisters of Cora, daughters of John P. K. Riblet, Riblet's grandfather: Ada Strome (whose death is recounted in chapter 5), Ida C. Riblet Keller, and Harriet Ella Riblet Ware.

2. Cyrius is a master of high order and one of Riblet's teachers. He appears only rarely.

3. What George is referring to specifically when he says "and since I'm working on the purple ray . . ." I can't be sure; "purple ray" is not explained in any of the material I have of Rib's. However, George does refer to the color purple, and also to gold, quite often, and as the two colors are generally symbolic of spirituality—spiritual power, in particular—it seems that we can take this purple ray reference in that light.

chapter 4

A New Mission and Trouble in the Heartland

1. Materialization was a relatively rare psychic phenomenon, more common in the latter part of the nineteenth century. The appearance of a body part—such as a hand or a face—or the entire body of a spirit appears to take form from a mass of ectoplasm, a white filmy

substance. For further discussion, see appendix 2, "Materialization."

Direct voice refers to a phenomenon in which, in the presence of certain mediums, spirits can speak in a voice that does not come from the medium.

2. A trumpet circle is a séance in which a trumpet—a lightweight tapered aluminum tube, perhaps thirty inches long, about one to six inches in diameter—is used to increase the volume of spirit voices, much as a megaphone does with human voices.

3. See endnote 1 above and also appendix 2, "Materialization," for information regarding ectoplasm.

4. Published by E. P. Dutton, New York, 1942. While on the earth plane, Betty White was a psychic and had experiences similar to Riblet's. Also like him, she felt unsure of her psychic abilities. After her unexpected passing, her husband, Stewart Edward White, wrote several books about her.

chapter 5

An Extraordinary Mystical Experience

1. Riblet's article was originally published in *The Light* magazine, in London, under his own name, Dr. Riblet B. Hout. It was later reprinted in *Reality Change*, vol. 1, no. 3 (Eugene, Oregon: SethNet Publishing, 1990).

chapter 6

The Astonished Healer

1. Clairvoyance is the ability to see without the use of the physical senses. Clairaudience is the ability to hear without the use of physical senses.

chapter 7

Reincarnation and the Pact

1. I have changed the names of the friends to whom Riblet refers here—except for his friend Charles—to protect their privacy.

chapter 8

Communication Between the Two Worlds

1. For further information on this type of spirit guidance, see appendix 3, "Rescue Circles."

chapter 9

Fate, Free Will, and a Visitor from a Higher Plane

1. The prisoner was not someone that Riblet knew in his physical lifetime. I have changed his name to Miller to protect his privacy.

2. Throughout the taped sessions, George often referred to Riblet as "the kid." And you'll notice that Jules Juret refers to him as "this child" and "the boy."

chapter 10

Soul Searching and Soul Growth

1. Originally published in 1970 by Prentice-Hall (Englewood Cliffs, NJ), *The Seth Material* was republished in 1995 by Buccaneer Books (Cutchogue, NY).

chapter 11

God and Gods in the Making

1. Benjamin Disraeli (1804–1881) was a British Prime Minister.

appendix 2

Materialization

1. Originally published in 1925, *The Facts of Psychic Science and Philosophy* was republished in 1959 (Secaucus, NJ: Carol Publishing Group).

2. Readers of Jane Roberts may be interested to note Jane's experience with ectoplasm. During her early psychic

research, with the help of the entity Seth, she materialized extra fingers during a séance. See chapter 3 of her book, *The Seth Material* (Englewood Cliffs, NJ: Prentice-Hall, 1970; reprint, Cutchogue, NY: Buccaneer Books, 1995).

appendix 3

Rescue Circles

1. New York: Doubleday, 1971; reprint, New York: Anchor Books, 1977.

2. *Thirty Years Among the Dead* was reprinted in 1996 by Health Research, Pomeroy, Washington.

Suggested Reading

Altea, Rosemary. *The Eagle and the Rose*. New York: Warner, 1996.

The Boy Who Saw True. Essex, England: C.W. Daniel, 1953; reprint, edited by Cyril Scott, Woodstock, NY: Beekman Publishers, 1989. This is the publication of a boy's diary. His name is not revealed.

Chesterfield Lives! Our First Hundred Years. Chesterfield, IN. Contact Camp Chesterfield, PO Box 132, Chesterfield, IN 46017; (765) 378-0236.

Crookall, Robert. *Out-of-the-Body Experiences: A Fourth Analysis of the Mystic Arts*. New York: University Books, 1970; reprint, Secausus, NJ: Citadel Press, 1992.

———. *The Study and Practice of Astral Projection*. Secausus, NJ: Citadel Press, 1960; reprint, 1983.

———. *The Supreme Adventure*. Cambridge, England: James Clarke & Co., 1961; reprint, Cambridge, England: Lutterworth Press, 1987.

Dahl, Lynda. *Beyond the Winning Streak: Using Conscious Creation to Consistently Win at Life*. Eugene, OR: Windsong, 1993. Now distributed by Moment Point Press.

Doyle, Sir Arthur Conan. *The History of Spiritualism*. Volumes 1 and 2. 1926; reprint, Manchester, NH: Ayer Publishing.

Friedman, Norman. *Bridging Science and Spirit: Common Elements in David Bohm's Physics, the Perennial Philosophy, and Seth*. Eugene, OR: Woodbridge Group, 1990. Now distributed by Moment Point Press.

Shakti Gawain. *Living in the Light: A Guide to Personal and Planetary Transformation*. Mill Valley, CA: Whatever Publishing, 1986; reprint, Novato, CA: New World Library, 1998.

Gelder, Dora van. *The Real World of Fairies: A First-Person Account*. 1904; reprint, Wheaton, IL: Theosophical Publishing House, 1977.

Guggenheim, William and Judith Guggenheim. *Hello From Heaven!* Longwood, FL: The ADC Project, 1995.

Hay, Louise. *You Can Heal Your Life*. Santa Monica, CA: Hay House, 1984; reprint, 1999.

Hodson, Geoffrey. *Fairies at Work and at Play*. Wheaton, IL: The Theosophical Publishing House, 1982.

Holms, A. Campbell. *The Facts of Psychic Science and Philosophy*. 1925. Now out of print and in the public domain.

Kubler-Ross, Elisabeth. *Death: The Final Stage of Growth*. Englewood Cliffs, NJ: Prentice-Hall, 1975; reprint, New York: Simon & Schuster, 1997.

LeShan, Lawrence. *The Medium, the Mystic, and the Physicist: Toward a General Theory of the Paranormal.* New York: Ballantine, 1975.

Millard, Joseph. *Edgar Cayce: Mystery Man of Miracles.* New York: Fawcett, 1956.

Moody, Raymond, Jr., M.D. *Life After Life: The Investigation of a Phenomenon—Survival of Bodily Death.* Covingtog, GA: Mockingbird Books, 1975; reprint, New York: Bantam, 1976.

Monroe, Robert A. *Journeys Out of the Body.* Garden City, NY: Doubleday, 1971; reprint, New York: Anchor Books, 1977.

————. *Far Journeys.* Garden City, NY: Doubleday, 1987.

Montgomery, Ruth. *Strangers Among Us.* New York: Coward, McCann & Geoghegan, 1979.

————. *A World Beyond: A Startling Message from the Eminent Psychic Arthur Ford from Beyond the Grave.* New York: Coward, McCann & Geoghegan, 1971; reprint, New York: Fawcett, 1989.

————. *The World Before.* New York: Coward, McCann & Geoghegan, 1976; reprint, New York: Fawcett, 1990.

Morse, Melvin, M.D. *Closer to the Light: Learning from Near-Death Experiences of Children.* New York: Ballantine Books, 1991.

Mossman, Tam. *Answers from a Grander Self.* Cave Creek, AZ: Tiger Maple Press, 1993.

Muldoon, Sylvan. *Case for Astral Projection.* Chicago: Aries Press, 1936.

Muldoon, Sylvan and Hereward Carrington. *The Projection of the Astral Body*. 1929; reprint, York, ME: Samuel Weiser, 1981.

Ring, Kenneth. *Lessons from the Light: What We Can Learn from the Near-Death Experience*. New York: Insight Books, 1998; reprint, Portsmouth, NH: Moment Point Press, 2000.

Roberts, Jane. *The God of Jane*. Englewood Cliffs, NJ: Prentice-Hall, 1981; new edition, with introduction by Susan M. Watkins, Portsmouth, NH: Moment Point Press, 2000.

———. *The Nature of Personal Reality: A Seth Book*. Englewood Cliffs, NJ: Prentice-Hall, 1974; reprint, San Rafael, CA: Amber-Allen, 1994.

———. *The Seth Material*. Englewood Cliffs, NJ: Prentice-Hall, 1970; reprint, Cutchogue, NY: Buccaneer Books, 1995.

Sugrue, Thomas. *There Is a River: The Story of Edgar Cayce*. New York: Henry Holt, 1942; reprinted as *The Story of Edgar Cayce: There is a River*, Virginia Beach, VA: A.R.E Press, 1997.

Swedenborg, Emanuel. *Awaken from Death*. Boston: J. Appleseed & Co., 1990.

Van Praagh, James. *Talking to Heaven: A Medium's Message of Life after Death*. New York: Penguin, 1997.

Walsch, Neale Donald. *Conversations with God: An Uncommon Dialogue*. Books 1–3. New York: G. P. Putnam's

Sons, 1996–98. (Book 1 originally published by Hampton Roads, 1995).

White, Stewart Edward. *The Unobstructed Universe.* New York: Dutton, 1940; reprint, Marble Hill, GA: Ariel Press, 1988.

———. *The Road I Know.* New York: Dutton, 1942.

———. *The Stars Are Still There.* New York: Dutton, 1946.

Wickland, Carl A., M.D. *Thirty Years Among the Dead.* 1924; reprint, Pomeroy, WA: Health Research, 1996.

Index

Bettilu Stein Faulkner was raised in Fort Wayne, Indiana, during the Great Depression—a time when her Uncle Riblet's visits provided a bright spot for her and her entire family. Bettilu is now a retired registered nurse and the mother of three grown children. She lives in Pennsylvania where she enjoys gardening, nutrition study, photography, and reading, among many other hobbies.

Other Great Titles from MOMENT POINT PRESS

LESSONS FROM THE LIGHT: What We Can Learn from the Near-Death Experience, by Kenneth Ring, Ph.D.

Kenneth Ring, cofounder of the International Association of Near-Death Studies, reveals the practical wisdom contained within the near-death experience. Considered by many to be the most important book on the subject. A must-read for anyone who has lost a loved one, or who fears his or her own death.

THE WISDOM CHRONICLES: An Everywoman's Awakening to Her Purpose, by Teri Harris Saa

Overworked, overwhelmed, and at her breaking point, an everywoman escapes life for a day and meets a mysterious teacher who changes her life. An excellent book for lively reading-group discussions.

THE GOD OF JANE, by Jane Roberts

Jane Roberts's Seth books have sold over 7.5 million copies worldwide. In *The God of Jane,* Roberts addresses many of the same issues and doubts that readers have had in trying to incorporate Seth's theories into their own lives. A personal and powerful book.

SPEAKING OF JANE ROBERTS: Remembering the Author of the Seth Material, by Susan M. Watkins

An intimate and insightful memoir that explores the life of Jane Roberts—her difficult childhood, her constant questioning of psychic abilities and sources of creativity, her resistance to Seth's advice, and her dramatic struggles with her health. Also offers a fascinating look at the complex relationship between two highly creative women.

CONSCIOUSLY CREATING EACH DAY: A 365-day perpetual calendar of spirited thought, edited by Susan Ray

Beloved voices both classic and contemporary—from religious figures to scientists, from poets to medical doctors—inspire us to transform our beliefs from limiting to limitless. Enjoy year after year. Makes a great gift.

For a complete catalog of titles, visit www.MomentPoint.com.
For special book-group rates, call 800-556-1828.